IMAGINING MIT

IMAGINING MIT

Designing a Campus for the Twenty-First Century

William J. Mitchell

Afterword by Charles M. Vest

The MIT Press   Cambridge, Massachusetts   London, England

MIT Press books may be purchased at special quantity discounts for business or sales promotional use. For information, please email special_sales@mitpress.mit.edu or write to Special Sales Department, The MIT Press, 55 Hayward Street, Cambridge, MA 02142.

This book was set in Bembo by the MIT Press.
Printed and bound in Spain.

Library of Congress Cataloging-in-Publication Data

Mitchell, William J. (William John), 1944-
    Imagining MIT : designing a campus for the twenty-first century / William J. Mitchell ; afterword by Charles M. Vest.
        p. cm.
    Includes bibliographical references and index.
    ISBN-13: 978-0-262-13479-8 (hc. : alk. paper)
1. Massachusetts Institute of Technology—Buildings. 2. Massachusetts Institute of Technology—Planning. 3. Campus planning—Massachusetts—Cambridge. I. Title.
T171.M49M58 2007
378.744'4—dc22

                              2006029824

CONTENTS

INTRODUCTION

When colleges and universities build, they don't just add to their inventories of floor space. They reveal—sometimes unwittingly—their prevailing values, aspirations, and preoccupations. Campuses are evolving, continually contested representations of the communities they house.

The late 1990s found the Massachusetts Institute of Technology with a grim, run-down campus that had earned it the nickname "the factory on the Charles," a huge pent-up demand for new space to accommodate its changing needs, and growing capacity to do something about it as a hot high-tech economy pumped funds into the endowment. The result was a decade-long, billion-dollar building boom that produced five major works of architecture—by Kevin Roche, Steven Holl, Frank Gehry, Charles Correa, and Fumihiko Maki. These and other projects added more than a million square feet of floor space, transformed the Institute's physical environment, and remade its relationship to adjacent communities.[1] They not only responded to immediate needs, but also became an expression of faith in the long-term future of the residential, campus-based university at a time when new communication technologies were raising questions about its continued relevance and alternative models—such as distance learning and international multi-campus universities—were emerging.[2] MIT, under President Charles Vest, was rebuilt as radically as Rome under Septimius Severus.

The process of campus reconstruction confronted MIT and its architects with the need to reflect critically on the very idea of a campus for a twenty-first-century research university, to engage a vigorous ongoing debate about principles of campus design, and to rethink the constituent building types. The outcome was a concrete realization—incomplete and imperfect, to be sure—of some compelling

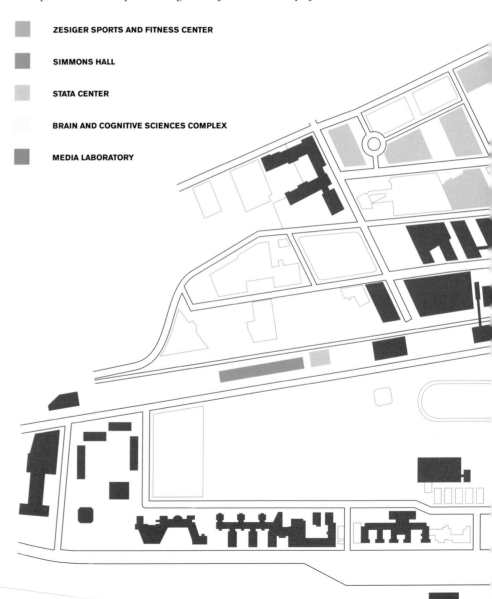

1 Map of the MIT campus showing five major architectural projects of the 1990s and 2000s.

ZESIGER SPORTS AND FITNESS CENTER

SIMMONS HALL

STATA CENTER

BRAIN AND COGNITIVE SCIENCES COMPLEX

MEDIA LABORATORY

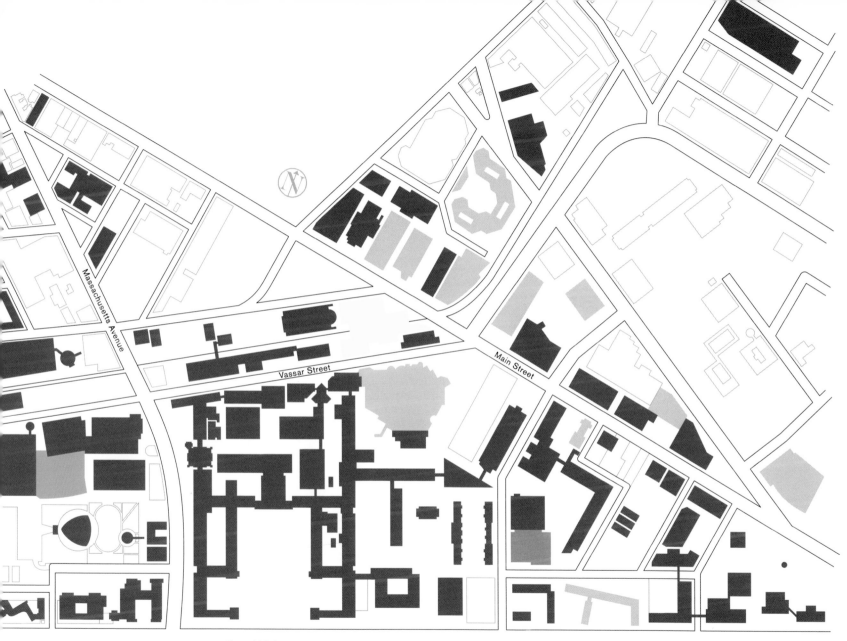

Massachusetts Avenue

Vassar Street

Main Street

Memorial Drive

ideas that emerged, were explored and argued about, and eventually took hold as the process unfolded. It illustrated both the opportunities and the difficulties of architectural production and city building under conditions of supercharged, technologically driven, entrepreneurial capitalism. And it disclosed the presence of significant ambiguities, contradictions, and cultural tensions within the MIT community—indeed, within the American academic world more generally—at the dawn of a new millennium.

This book critically examines both the built results and the complex processes leading to them. It is a story of architects and their buildings, but not only that. It departs from the standard, mythic form of an architectural narrative—the tale of a heroic designer and enlightened patron overcoming adversity to realize a vision—to develop a *Rashomon*-like construction of multiple voices and viewpoints. It tells not only of architectural intentions and inventions, but also of money, politics, institutional dynamics, project management, and ideological and cultural contention. My own text provides an engaged insider's account—written from my perspective, during this period, as dean of the School of Architecture and Planning and architectural advisor to MIT's president.[3] The various architects are represented by their drawings, models, and computer graphics, and by their own words. Emeritus President Vest, who, in his institutional role, initiated and led the effort, contributes a candidly reflective afterword.[4]

The illustrations show not only the evolution of each project, but also the relationship of diverse and evolving architectural representation techniques—sketching, drafting, scale modeling, prototyping, photographic and digital imaging, mathematical modeling of engineering systems, and eventually three-dimensional computer modeling and rendering—to the conception, discussion, and development of architectural ideas. Design media do not directly determine architec-

tural possibilities, but in general, architects build what they can represent and represent what they can build. Over time, the repertoire of available techniques has expanded, and this has opened up new domains of potential building forms for consideration. To clarify this connection, I have confined the illustrations to contemporary representations of projects, and I have taken care to show how different types of representations play their characteristic roles at different stages in the lengthy processes of floating, exploring, developing and detailing, and documenting design concepts.

This is, in the end, a story not only of successfully completed projects, but also of rejected options, regretted compromises, and unrealized proposals. Designing a building is a messy, informally structured generate-and-test process; framed by the cultural conditions of the moment, the architect's wide-ranging imagination proposes, while some combination of institutional and economic imperatives, emerging exigencies, and sheer accident disposes. It is the social exploration of a complex, shifting solution space. The construction of today's MIT campus has actualized just one politically and economically contingent path through a maze of might-have-beens, and the paths projected but then not taken are as interesting and revealing as those that were.

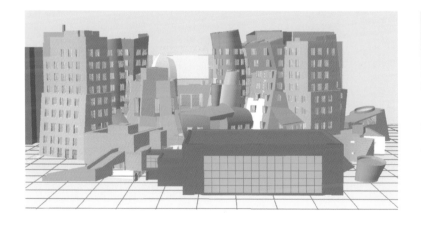

2 Representation techniques employed in the Stata design and construction process: sketches, physical scale models, three-dimensional digital model, and CAD/CAM construction.

IMAGINING MIT

Ancient universities like Cambridge are tightly woven into the fabrics of the cities that contain them. A few modern universities follow the same pattern; New York University, for example, is inseparably intertwined with Greenwich Village. But it has been more usual, in North America, for a university to take the form of a campus—a discrete, clearly bounded parcel of land with a master-planned collection of buildings and open spaces. Access to the campus may be controlled by walls, gates, and traffic checkpoints. And separation from the surrounding city may be legal as well as physical; many campuses are exempt from local property taxes and building codes, and even operate their own police forces. After a visit to America in the 1930s, Le Corbusier observed in some astonishment: "Each college or university is an urban unit in itself, a small or large city. But a green city. . . . The American university is a world in itself."[v]

The word "campus" has a resonantly Roman sound that must have appealed to the classically educated founders of the earliest American colleges and universities. The English term derives, of course, from the Latin for field—as in the Campus Martius, the Roman field devoted to games, athletic practice, and military drills. It carries intimations of the provisional and the reconfigurable—of camps and campgrounds, and of spaces for contest and combat. According to the *Oxford English Dictionary*, it was first used, in its current sense, to refer to Princeton.[6]

The patterns of the modern academic campus have dual origins in the seventeenth century and earlier; some of them can be traced back to the European college quadrangle, and some to the colonial American practice of arranging freestanding residential and civic

I consider the common plan, followed in this country but not in others, of making one large and expensive building, as unfortunately erroneous. It is infinitely better to erect a small and separate lodge for each separate professorship, with only a hall below for his class, and two chambers above for himself; joining these lodges by barracks for a certain portion of the students, opening into a covered way to give a dry communication between all the schools. The whole of these arranged around an open square of grass and trees, would make it, what it should be in fact, an academical village.
—THOMAS JEFFERSON

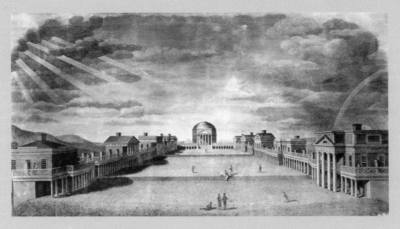

1 Thomas Jefferson's "academical village" at the University of Virginia, as it appeared in the 1820s: detail of University of Virginia map by Herman Böÿe, 1827.

buildings around a village green.[7] It was Thomas Jefferson, in his design for the University of Virginia, around 1820, who first demonstrated how to combine them in a compelling new way.[8] Jefferson placed a grassy rectangle at the center of the grounds (he didn't call it a campus, and at Virginia they still don't), a monumental, Pantheon-like rotunda at the head of that open space, and colonnaded residential wings with embedded pavilions on either side.

Formally, Jefferson's design fused the received pattern of pavilions facing a green with that of the open-ended quadrangle. Functionally, it combined living space and teaching space around a unifying public space. It was not only a brilliant piece of practical planning, but also a passionate expression of humanistic ideals in a consistent, sophisticated (if sometimes eccentric) architectural language derived ultimately from Palladio.

This appropriation of Renaissance forms, however, entailed some telling functional shifts. In the Italian prototypes, the central structure was a landowner's villa; in Jefferson's hands it became a library. The farmyard that it fronted became a formal public space. The *barchessi* on either side, which in the Veneto had sheltered farm animals, now housed Virginia's professors and students. And there were slaves in the basement.

You can read the subsequent history of American campus design as a series of footnotes to Jefferson. His "academical village" prototype has turned out to be remarkably robust and adaptable, with endless capacity for transformation, augmentation, and hybridization to accommodate new components and systems—from automobiles and parking structures to wet labs, teaching hospitals, football stadiums, childcare centers, nuclear reactors, lab animal facilities, computer networks, coed dorms, high-rise towers, European modernism, wheelchair ramps, Frisbees, fast food, and mechanical equipment in the basement. It has continued to serve as campus populations have grown from a few hundred to thousands or tens of thousands, and as institutions have subdivided internally into schools and departments. It has evolved, in different ways under different pressures, to serve the needs of private and public universities, small liberal arts colleges and great research institutions, cozy rural retreats and sprawling multiversities. Not surprisingly, though, America's numerous post-Jefferson campuses have rarely had the crisp clarity of conception and execution of the original—and when occasionally they did, they didn't stay that way for long.

Typically, today's campuses have grown from cores of original buildings that were organized according to some local interpretation of the Jeffersonian model—if not always executed in the same classical style. Often, the original campus buildings now house the president's office, serve as ivied heritage theme parks providing a "freshman experience," and—like Main Street and Snow White's Castle at Disneyland—establish a brand image. But, as campuses have expanded outward over time, they have developed into complex collages of diverse architectural elements, open spaces, carparks, and circulation systems.

Generally, they have not been built for powerful patrons who knew their minds and could get exactly what they wanted, but have resulted instead from extended, contentious political processes among squabbling stakeholders whose instincts and interests often diverged: students, faculty, senior administrators, managers, trustees, alumni, donors, federal funding agencies, federal and state legislators, local community groups, and local government. They express not only lofty ideals, but also the grubby exigencies of land acquisition, construction financing, and the ceaseless pursuit of gifts, research funding streams, and AAA bond ratings.[9] They record the interpretations and reinter-

pretations of the genius loci by successive architects and planners who have brought different sensibilities and predilections to their tasks. They are traces cast in brick and stone—and, more recently, in steel, concrete, and glass—of shifts in intentions and values, inconsistencies and contradictions that have never been resolved, arguments won and lost, ideas that worked out and ones that didn't.

Interpreted in terms of cultural politics, the control of building and urban form has usually been a victor's spoil in one of the endless internal battles waged over a university's inherent, irreconcilable contradictions. There are plenty of exceptions, ironies, and paradoxes to observe in this, but it is easy to sketch some general mappings from ideology to bricks and mortar. The primacy of tradition is mostly celebrated by continuing to build in approximations to the style of the founding fathers (no matter that those revered forebears had often exhibited obnoxious prejudices, and had generally excluded women and ethnic and religious minorities), while a commitment to innovation and progressive social policy is represented by iconoclastic modernism. Belief in stable core values—and brand-led marketing—sits comfortably with consistency of style and materials, while the embrace of difference and diversity suggests correspondingly more complex and fragmented architectural responses. Engineering rationality favors inexpensive, pragmatically organized workspace, while the arts and humanities view architecture as a cultural enterprise concerned with representation and symbolic nuance. Conceiving of the university as a retreat from the world yields lots of walls, gates, and secluded quadrangles, while greater engagement with it generates a more permeable campus of streets and public spaces.

Whatever might be suggested by the prescriptions of theorists with axes to grind, the golden-hazed memoirs of aged alumni, the carefully crafted texts of student recruiting materials, the glossy brochures for capital campaigns, and the idyllic images on the splash pages of websites, American campuses are not clear, consistent realizations of ideas that were specified by visionaries and frozen in place at particular historic moments. They are unstable, evolving registrations of the messy, imperfect, disputatious life that unfolds within them.

MIT's Cambridge campus—which replaced the Institute's original buildings in the Back Bay area of Boston—has been a contested patch of ground from the beginning.[10] After an offer by Harvard University to take over the Institute's debts and move it to the Harvard campus to replace its own Lawrence Scientific School had been debated by the faculty and rejected, the New Tech was built on fill that had been dumped into the wetlands of the Charles River. The site had been intended for residential use, and was gridded with streets like Back Bay across the river, but the area was surrounded by factories, tenement houses, and railway lines, so it was not attractive to potential buyers and residential development never took off. In 1912 MIT's president Richard Maclaurin negotiated to purchase the land from the city of Cambridge for $775,500—$500,000 of which was contributed by Thomas Coleman du Pont. In return, Maclaurin rather rashly promised—only to be unable to keep his word in the end—that the first building on the site would be a chemistry laboratory.

As the site selection and acquisition process ground on, a debate got under way about design principles, style, decision-making process, and who should get the architectural work. A spontaneous, informal architectural competition developed. Someone (it isn't clear who) fired a shrewd preemptive shot in 1911 by publishing, in *Technology Review*, an unsigned drawing showing a Georgian Revival campus laid out on Jeffersonian principles, with a central lawn and domed administration building. Stephen Child, a civil engineering alumnus and former superintendent of the sewer department of the nearby city of Newton, jumped in with a formal proposal—along much the same lines, and a pragmatic response to the program of space needs, but

The time is fast going by for the great personal or individual achievement of any one man standing alone and without the help of those around him. And the time is coming when all great things will be done by that type of cooperation in which each man performs the function for which he is best suited, each man preserves his own individuality and is supreme in his particular function, and each man at the same time loses none of his originality and proper personal initiative, and yet is controlled by and must work harmoniously with many other men.
—FREDERICK WINSLOW TAYLOR

1 Terra nullius: the site for the future New Tech in 1910—created by dumping landfill in the tidal marshes of the Charles River, in the days before environmental concerns began to discourage such practices.

2 A Beaux-Arts proposal for the New Tech by Désiré Despradelle, with a grand axis running from a Charles River landing on the formal, elegant Boston side to a smokestack on the industrial Cambridge side. This and other early proposals established the idea that the campus should formally front the Charles River.

architecturally cruder—a few days after the site had been acquired. Probably horrified by this, the brilliant architecture professor Désiré Despradelle responded with a series of elegant Beaux-Arts schemes that would not have been out of place in some grand European capital. Ralph Adams Cram, with romance in his soul and breathtaking insouciance about practicalities, proposed an Isola Bella of engineering on an island in the Charles.

Things got serious when Maclaurin raised a gift of $2,500,000 from George Eastman of Eastman Kodak. The civil engineering alumnus and Corporation member John Ripley Freeman quickly counseled against engaging an architect, and instead got himself hired to conduct a needs study based on the ideas advanced in his friend Frederick Winslow Taylor's *Principles of Scientific Management* (1911)— an influential text that emphasized division of labor, science in place of rule of thumb, cooperation and coordination, minimization of wasted effort, and maximization of output.[11] Freeman meticulously analyzed hundreds of precedents in Taylorist terms, and eventually produced a proposal of his own. Rather than an assemblage of Jeffersonian pavilions in which a professor "reigns undisturbed, largely in a little kingdom of his own," it was a million square feet in a "single connected group closely resembling the arrangement of the best modern factories." The plan diagrammed the division of scientific and engineering effort, as conceived at the time. For efficient circulation and "avoidance of unnecessary traffic" it was tied together by double-loaded corridors. For construction efficiency and flexibility the structure had a strictly modular reinforced concrete frame and lightweight partitions that could easily be moved. For light and air, there was a protomodern glass curtain wall. For architectural propriety and a grudging nod to tradition, there was a skin of classical detailing, a colonnaded green (awkwardly displaced to one side), and a flattened-out dome.

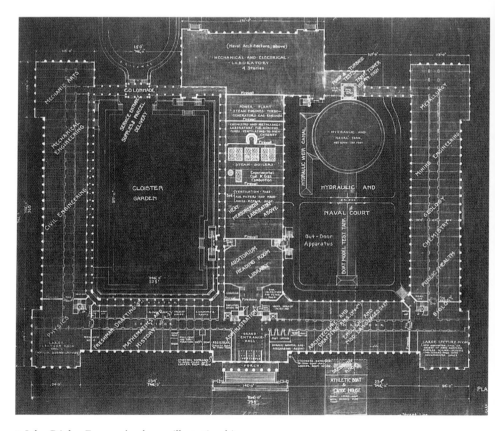

3 John Ripley Freeman's scheme, illustrating his Taylorist conception of the efficient division and coordination of academic labor under one roof.

4 Perspective of Freeman's scheme, relentlessly demonstrating the idea that there should be one massive building in a consistent classical style. Done in concrete as proposed, it would have been a grim, intimidating, mill-like presence confronting old Boston across the Charles.

Motives

(1) An abundance of window light and a flood of controlled ventilation and filtered air.

(2) Maximum economy in energy and time of students and instructors.

(3) Maximum economy in cost of efficient service in heating, ventilating, janitor service and general maintenance.

(4) Maximum resistance to fire, decay and wear.

(5) Maximum economy in cost of building per square foot of useful floor space.

(6) Architectural details and outlines derived from the Greek Classic style, which have satisfied the human eye for 2000 years—modifying the windows as needed for science study as contrasted with the dim religious light of a temple.

(7) A simple dominating mass with uniform cornice height which shall invite attention from the many thousands who daily cross the basin over the two great bridges.

Concrete and steel, being the leading building materials of the present epoch, appear peculiarly appropriate for the construction of the New Technology.

—JOHN RIPLEY FREEMAN

Freeman's project, with its aggressive claims to scientifically grounded transcendence of outmoded tradition, appears retrospectively as one in a series of twentieth-century rationalized campus plans—from Henry Hornbostel's wonderful blend of the Beaux-Arts and the industrial at Carnegie Mellon to Candilis-Josic-Woods's mat-plan, steel-framed Berlin Free University. But it was not one of the triumphs. Mostly, it failed to resolve the contradiction between the residual imagery of a bucolic academical village and the spatial organization of an efficient urban research factory. The MIT Executive Committee rejected it, and asked the prominent architecture alumnus Cass Gilbert to produce a new scheme. Gilbert was understandably reluctant to work with the increasingly frustrated and cranky Freeman, and after some negotiation he declined. Not one to give up easily, Freeman responded with an offer to complete the project for "one half of the regular architectural fee." To resolve a growing nightmare of Corporation-level politics, and on the advice of John D. Rockefeller Jr., Maclaurin sent Freeman packing and turned to yet another accomplished architecture graduate—William Welles Bosworth, designer of the corporate headquarters of AT&T.

Bosworth got the job in February 1913, and produced his scheme by the summer. It was the graceful synthesis of rationally planned interiors and classical clothing that had eluded Freeman. Construction of what is now known as the Main Complex quickly began, and continued in stages until the years of the Second World War.

In its layout and massing, Bosworth's Main Complex is a glorious, unified, urban-scale composition in the high Beaux-Arts manner—one that creates a dramatic presence on the Charles River, and easily holds its own with Harvard's monuments on one side and the Boston Public Library and the Museum of Fine Arts on the other. It seamlessly works in a Palladian/Jeffersonian dome and a rectangular central

5 William Welles Bosworth (front and center, with clasped hands) in his studio with his staff.

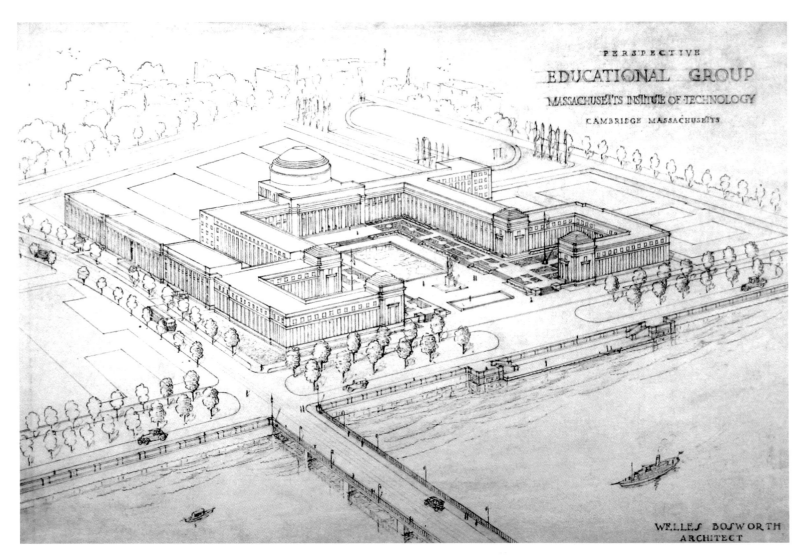

PERSPECTIVE

EDUCATIONAL GROUP

MASSACHUSETTS INSTITUTE OF TECHNOLOGY

CAMBRIDGE MASSACHUSETTS

WELLES BOSWORTH
ARCHITECT

6 Bosworth's scheme for the Main Complex. (Note how the Cambridge
context is veiled by a flurry of vaguely indicated vegetation.)

7 A construction photograph of Bosworth's Main Complex, compared to a
watercolor rendering, reveals the modular, concrete-framed system beneath
the classical limestone skin.

green. In its exterior details it deploys classical motifs with the erudite subtlety appropriate to a great center of learning. Inside, though, it is all Frederick Winslow Taylor and John Ripley Freeman; it has double-loaded corridors—the famous "infinite corridor" system—modular rectangular bays, reinforced concrete framing, and non-structural partitions that have accommodated many changes in space use and interior layout over the years. And, around the back, it is yellow brick and industrial metal-framed windows.

Bosworth's planning also shows the vivid influence of the eighteenth-century French architectural theorist Jean-Nicolas-Louis Durand.[12] Durand's well-known textbooks, with which Bosworth must have been familiar, demonstrated endless ways of assembling rectangular modules around long axes to form vast, symmetrical, classically clad buildings that could accommodate the new space needs of an industrializing, urbanizing era. They provided, in effect, a generative grammar for large-scale classical architecture. Bosworth—a Francophile, and a smooth operator who understood the aspirations of his moneyed patrons—would have realized that an update of Durand was the perfect formula for an early twentieth-century America that was robustly confident in its science and industry, but still looked to Europe when it came to culture.

The choice of exterior style was an exercise in what we would now recognize as academic branding. The basic options were Georgian, Gothic, and Neoclassical—each carrying its own symbolic baggage. (Californian campuses also had the possibilities of Spanish Colonial, Lombardic, and other warm-weather styles.) Georgian, as at Harvard, harked back to the colonial era. Gothic made reference to the medieval universities of Europe. And Bosworth's choice of Neoclassical evoked Jefferson, the European Enlightenment, and the intellectual heritage of Greece and Rome. The institutional identity that this established was

8 Application of the classically detailed limestone skin to the concrete frame.

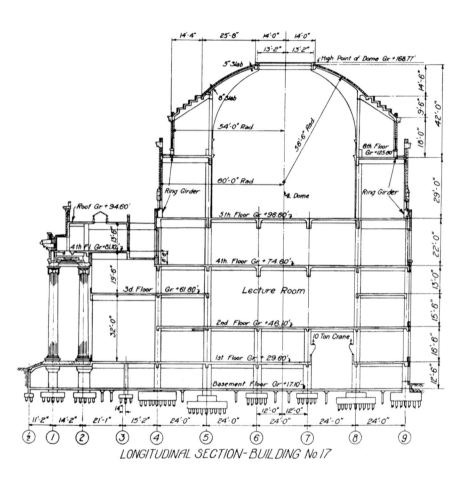

LONGITUDINAL SECTION-BUILDING No 17

9 Section through the dome, with lecture hall below. The exterior implies a tall, Pantheon-like space, but when you enter there is no evidence of it. The rotunda is much smaller than the exterior suggests, it occupies just the top floors, and can only be reached by elevators and narrow stairs.

10 The dome under construction.

11 The library reading room under the dome—before its character was altered by an unsympathetic renovation.

reinforced by inscription of the names of scientific and engineering heroes (some now forgotten) around the cornices.

If you approach from the Charles River side, the partially Jeffersonian lineage of Bosworth's scheme is immediately evident. But the deviations from the ancestor's form and functioning—as in diagrams showing the evolutionary origins of species—are even more startling. The wings on either side have become massive, so that the three-sided courtyard (now known as Killian Court, and the site of commencement exercises) loses any hint of the Palladian barnyard and *barchessi* and reads instead as a grand *cour d'honneur* reminiscent of those at Versailles and Buckingham Palace. They consist not of residential space, but of laboratories and offices. And their generous scale was originally justified not by the political imperative of expressing regal splendor, but by the need to accommodate large laboratory machines.

The great court, looking out across the Charles River to the Boston skyline, was meant to serve as MIT's main entrance. It has a grand entry hall on axis, offices for the president and other senior administrators at the location usually reserved for the monarch's bed-chamber, and secondary entries symmetrically disposed on either side. Some renderings even show the court continuing to a stepped river landing for dramatic arrivals by water. But it was not in a convenient location, so when Bosworth added a second stage to the Main Complex in the 1930s, he included a new main entrance, with grandiose steps and a dome to signify its status, at 77 Massachusetts Avenue. As a result of this shift, the east-west corridor linking the two domes now became the main circulation spine—the Main Corridor of the infinite corridor system. For generations of students this dim, crowded passageway, flanked by doors of brown woodwork and frost-ed glass, seemed the most unforgettable architectural feature of the campus—MIT's equivalent of Harvard Yard but, in its grim way,

12 The Great War face of MIT: watercolor rendering of Killian Court (with the unexecuted statue of Minerva), and a photograph taken soon after completion.

maybe even more memorable. The planned major feature had not worked out as intended, and an almost accidental by-product of changing circumstance had usurped its place.

The Main Complex was unmistakably conceived of as a monument to the industrial technology of its time—particularly the chemical industry, as represented by DuPont and Eastman Kodak—but chemistry and chemical engineering eventually moved out to more up-to-date laboratories on its periphery. The great machines are now long gone—either consigned to nondescript sheds on the industrial outskirts of the campus or replaced by computers and software. Beneath the unchanging skin, the vast interior has passed through a cycle of functional centrality and intensive use followed by obsolescence, disinvestment and diminishing activity. At the time of the Vietnam War and countercultural protest, architecture students filled the growing void by occupying the floor space around 77 Massachusetts Avenue with ad hoc, *favella*-like constructions that proposed a radical alternative to Taylorist spatial organization and classical grandeur. Then it gentrified. As the virtues of central real estate, flexible and accommodating floor space, large windows, and high ceilings were appreciated once again, ambitious deans and department heads increasingly saw it as a site for space acquisition, rehabilitation, and development for new uses. These processes have transformed the totalizing clarity of its original functional diagram into the multilayered diversity and complexity of mature urban fabric. Only the president's office, looking out over Killian Court, has remained as Bosworth long ago imagined it.

Bosworth's project, through its choice of planning and construction principles, sent an unambiguous signal of where MIT was headed. Over two centuries, American campus planners have been evolving the Jeffersonian genotype in two radically different directions. Where the liberal arts are central, and mostly in suburban and rural contexts—magnificently at Wellesley College, for example—campuses have typically developed as collections of modestly scaled pavilions and occasional towers in parkland. You walk from building to building beneath the trees. Where the big-money, laboratory-based enterprises of large-scale science, engineering, and medicine are dominant, however, buildings have generally grown larger and fused together into monolithic masses, now interconnected not by airy colonnades but by internal corridors, bridges, and tunnels; you can inhabit them without ever going outside. In large, comprehensive universities you can find various uneasy mixtures. At UCLA, for instance, there is a romantic northern campus of pavilions for the arts and humanities—very Nathanael West—fading out into the leafy hills of Bel Air, and there is a southern campus of vast, interconnected complexes for the engineering and medical schools, engaging the endless grid of the Los Angeles Basin. For Bosworth, though, the direction was never in doubt; his Main Complex stands in explicit opposition to the Jeffersonian "academical village" as a confident, pioneering expression of the idea of campus as urban megastructure.

Down with architecture as boring originality! You can say Michelangelo and Palladio were "good rather than original." What they built was not "signature," it was not egocentric, it was *good*.

And what about my love for the original MIT buildings, the great complex? Someone might say, "Well, that's what you've been arguing against, isn't it?" On the outside it is very much an iconic, grandiose kind of gesture. But on the inside it is just an amazingly down-to-earth, vernacular industrial space of that period. It can accommodate non-distracting environment, and flexibility over time for different uses—changes that can happen spatially as well as mechanically, and most recently electronically. It's a transvestite kind of building, wearing clothes that are different from the body inside.

–ROBERT VENTURI

13 Sketch by Robert Venturi, in 2002, of a proposal for rebuilding Bosworth's Main Corridor in response to twenty-first-century needs.

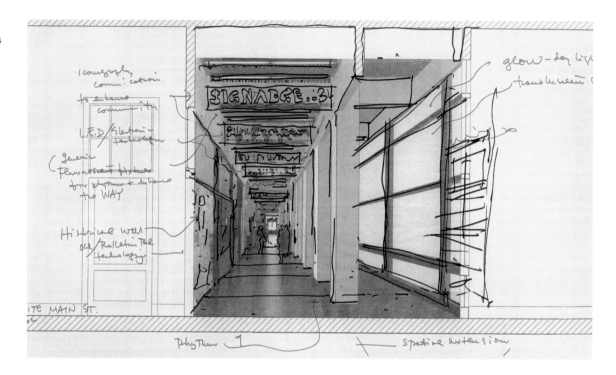

In the postwar years, with Bosworth finally gone from the scene, old Europe exhausted and in ruins, and American technology and industry in the ascendant, the intentions and conditions that had generated the Main Complex no longer prevailed. Building 20, which had been erected to house the Radiation Laboratory's war efforts, was a prefabricated, modular building that made no gestures at all to the Beaux-Arts or indeed to architecture as an affair of history and culture at all.[13] It was Durand with the classical skin ruthlessly stripped away. And its modest, generic spaces proved to be remarkably accommodating; after their war service, they adapted to incubating computer science, artificial intelligence, cognitive science, Chomskian linguistics, and crude LSD-inspired murals by Timothy Leary.

When its wartime mission was complete, the Radiation Laboratory simply closed down. But, before they left the building, the Rad Lab researchers spent six months documenting the technical content of their work in 27 dense volumes.[14] These publications established a new foundation for electrical engineering—and ultimately engineering in general—by grounding it in scientific first principles rather than field experience and handbook rules and charts. In the same spirit, *Science: The Endless Frontier,* Vannevar Bush's famous 1947 report to President Truman, proposed the idea of the National Science Foundation, which was eventually established in 1950.[15] An intellectual revolution that had largely begun in Building 20 quickly changed the organization of scientific and engineering research in the United States, the curricula of engineering schools,[16] and the funding of buildings at research universities. The demands generated by the Cold War and the launch of Sputnik pumped increasing funding into the new

1 The World War II face of MIT: Building 20, home of the Radiation Laboratory.

system. Under it, federal research sponsoring agencies supported not only the direct costs of research, but also the associated indirect costs of employee benefits, graduate student tuition, equipment, and research space. With the funding came strict regulation—in architecture, as in everything else—of what could be charged to the federal government. If you couldn't charge it, then it probably wouldn't get built.

Building 20's no-nonsense pragmatism had comported well enough with the machine-age modernism espoused by a new generation of European architects who had fled the Nazis and ended up in influential positions at American schools—including Harvard and MIT. As MIT adapted to the new federal funding system and its great era of postwar expansion unfolded as a result, the planners and architects of its many new laboratories took these cues.[17] They retained the

2 Interior of Building 20, site of wartime radar research.

3 A vision of the Cold War face of MIT: perspective of the Bush Building, designed by Walter Netsch of Skidmore, Owings & Merrill. Netsch proposed a modular, extensible, system-built structure of Shokbeton precast concrete, but this was rejected as too expensive. The concrete frame was actually poured in place, and wood was substituted for concrete for the window frames. The poorly built structure has subsequently deteriorated.

4 The Bush Building, as completed in 1965. Its spacious central lobby was intended to serve as MIT's main entrance from the north, but budgets and circumstances were against it; two of the four elevator shafts were left empty, escalators up to the Main Complex were eliminated from the design, the proposed grand entrance court remained a clutter of minor buildings and service roads, and the anticipated crowds of pedestrians never materialized. A proposal to extend it five bays to the east, and thus create a consistent, modern northern face for the Main Complex, was never implemented.

principles of modularity, the double-loaded corridor layout with standardized dimensions, connectivity, and arrangement of linear buildings to form bounded open spaces. But they did away with Bosworth's classical facades and domes, and substituted a stripped-down modernist exterior idiom of glass curtain walls, exposed concrete, and yellow brick panels. And, to satisfy the funding agencies, they were careful to maximize net-to-gross floor space ratios.

The effect of all the new laboratory building was to expand Bosworth's web of structures, corridors, and courtyards to the east and north, forming an increasingly imposing edge along Vassar Street—reminiscent of the Old Brick Row at Yale and its numerous successors, but without the picturesque charm, and facing a railway line and industrial installations rather than an open green. Instead of being developed as green quadrangles that evoked the pastoral ideals of earlier American campuses, many of the spaces between the buildings became service yards and parking lots. As MIT expanded into industrial Cambridge, industrial Cambridge infiltrated MIT.

Although the money for this expansion came largely from the federal government—with attendant bureaucratic framing and cost accounting of architectural projects—MIT's connections to business and industry were not forgotten, and the architectural work was mostly done by large corporate practices. Occasionally the results were distinguished, particularly in the case of I. M. Pei's essays in crisply detailed concrete, and Harry Ellenzweig's consistently shrewd and sensitive interventions, but mostly they were not. Without Bosworth's cultured urbanity to enliven it, the simplistic extension of the system that Freeman's rationalizing had established was producing far too many prosaic and dingy spaces. By the 1990s, when the opportunity presented itself, it was clearly time to rethink.

Meanwhile, across the road from the 77 Massachusetts Avenue entrance, a shadow campus organized according to very different principles was emerging. It was the work of two extraordinary architects with their cultural roots in Finland—Alvar Aalto and Eero Saarinen.

In a move that paralleled those of the Europeans Ludwig Mies van der Rohe to the Illinois Institute of Technology and Walter Gropius to Harvard, Aalto started to come to MIT to teach in 1940 and continued his visits until 1945. He wasn't the sort of hire that human resources likes; it turned out that he drank a lot, was struggling with family problems, and didn't stay long. But he had already established himself as one of the revered heroes of twentieth-century modernism, and he was an unforgettable inspiration to a generation of professors and students while he was at the Institute. And a talented and determined dean of architecture, William Wurster, made sure that his star professor got the commission to design a new dormitory, Baker House, on Memorial Drive overlooking the Charles. Wurster was an important modernist himself, and an admirer of Aalto's warm humanism; he certainly wanted no part of a chilly and grandiose neoclassicism that now not only seemed absurdly retrograde, but had also been thoroughly discredited through its adoption by Hitler's architect Albert Speer.

Furthermore, new theory was in the air in the 1940s. Writing in *Architectural Forum* in 1947, for example, the Harvard modernist Joseph Hudnut attacked the idea of campuses as "grand compositions . . . corseting the body of a live and unpredictable creature." Instead, he proposed: "We must set them free to develop their environment in whatever way may best suit their existing needs. . . . Let's imagine the university, as the city planners imagine the city, as a growing organism whose form lies partly in the past, partly in the future. . . . If we make a master plan then, it must be in such general terms as will admit of new interpretations and unexpected development. We can take nothing for granted."[18] This process-oriented view was far more realistic in a rapidly changing postwar world. It opened the way to critical reexamination of the idea of a campus, and to architectural innovation. In less creative hands, though, it was to have the unintended effect of shifting the focus of campus planning from place and community to a bureaucratic, reductionist process of capital planning and budgeting, real estate acquisition, project development, and facility management.

Baker House, completed and occupied in 1949, is an undoubted masterpiece that deliberately inverts just about every principle of the Main Complex. It is not part of a continuous web of buildings and quadrangles, but a freestanding block. Its corridors do not run through a deep interior but have lots of daylight. Its main stairway is not neatly tucked into the grid, but flies up the exterior in a manner that recalls Russian Constructivism. It is not neoclassically axial and symmetrical in its composition, but curves sinuously on one side in response to the river and deploys planes and right angles on the other in response to the street grid. Its materials—red brick, wooden window frames, and occasional stone—are warm and natural rather than neutral and institutional. Its structural systems and materials are exposed, not concealed beneath a historicist stone facing. It doesn't simply replicate the colors, textures, and motifs of its architectural context, but responds critically to them to produce something that is related but different, and of its own cultural moment. When it was finished, it succeeded in establishing a powerful *new* context that has since been

WESTERN UNION
TELEGRAM

BB271

B CDU621 105/104 PD INTL=CD HELSINKI VIA RCA 5 1751

=LT DEAN BURCHARD=

MIT CAMBRIDGE (MASS)

=DEAR JOHN JUST UNABLE TO PRODUCE ENOUGH ARCHITECTURAL
PHILOSOPHY YOU MAY PUBLISH THIS TELEGRAMLETTER AS A
SUBSTITUTE STOP SIBELIUS SAID IF YOU PUBLISH THREE WORDS
OF EXPLAINING MUSIC AT LEAST TWO WORDS ARE WRONG THIS
MAY BE TRUE ALSO IN MY ARCHITECTURAL PHILOSOPHY STOP IN=

WESTERN UNION
TELEGRAM

(06).

=B CDU621/2

=ORDINARY DISCUSSION IN RECENT DECADES THE TRADITIONALLY
IMITATION HAS BEEN POINTED OUT AS MAIN ENEMY OF
CONTEMPORARY ART I THINK HOWEVER THE ENEMY NUMBER ONE
TODAY IS MODERN FORMALISM NON TRADITIONAL WHERE IN HUMAN
ELEMENTS ARE DOMINATING STOP TRUE ARCHITECTURE THE REAL
THING IS ONLY WHERE MAN STANDS IN CENTRE=

BEST REGARDS YOURS ALVAR=

1 Alvar Aalto explains his architectural philosophy
in a telegram to MIT dean John Burchard.

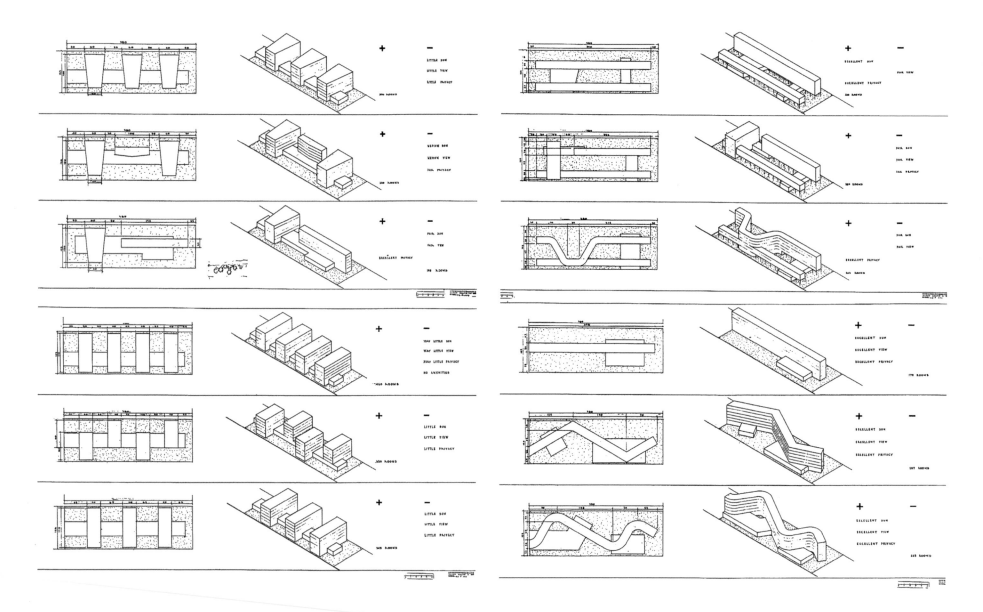

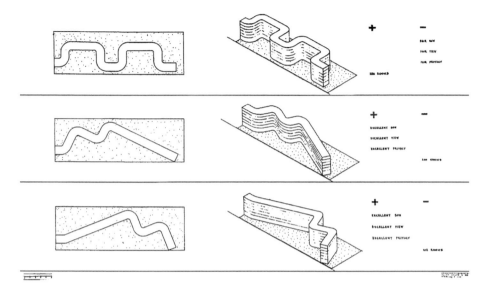

2 Aalto's meticulous massing studies—comparing options in terms of sun, view, and privacy—for Baker House.

extended with additional dormitory buildings along the river—but not, unfortunately, with the same questioning spirit or artistry.

It is a modest, unpretentious building that derives its striking effects not from grandeur and historical allusion but—representing the best of the modernist spirit—from sensitive attention to everyday human needs and pleasures, careful interrelation of private and social spaces to create a sense of community, clear expression of the properties of materials and structural systems, and response to the imperatives of natural light, natural cross-ventilation, and views of the river. Its form is breathtakingly beautiful, and creates astonishingly varied effects of shading and shadow, but Aalto's meticulous diagrams and analyses of massing options demonstrated that (at least in his mind) form followed function—that the chosen arrangement provided better light, views, and privacy than more pedestrian options.

Following the triumph of Aalto (not one, incidentally, that was universally acclaimed on campus), and after several architects had explored master-plan ideas for the site, Eero Saarinen was commissioned to design a new quadrangle across from 77 Massachusetts Avenue. Saarinen was an adventurous innovator, and came from outside the circle of MIT architecture professors and graduates, but he had the sort of track record that gives comfort to selection committees and administrators who have their jobs on the line. His father Eliel had migrated from Finland to create one of the world's great campuses for the Cranbrook Academy of Art near Detroit, and Eero had grown up there to become an architectural prodigy. He is principally remembered today as the designer of large-scale projects for leading corporations of postwar America—General Motors, John Deere, TWA, CBS, and IBM—and for his university projects.

The building opportunity was provided by Sebastian S. Kresge, a wealthy and particularly strong-minded benefactor of MIT. Unlike

3 Model of Baker House.

4 Ezra Stoller's photographs of Baker House soon after completion. Ezra Stoller © Esto.

5 A Baker House room in the 1940s. Ezra Stoller © Esto.

the turn-of-the-century industrialists who had bankrolled the creation of Bosworth's Main Campus, Kresge had made his money in the midcentury retail sector—the Kresge discount stores, predecessors of Kmart. Kresge funded the chapel and the auditorium that bear his name. It is not likely that they would otherwise have risen to the top of the Building Committee's priority list. Where Bosworth's megastructure consists of embedded and numbered buildings, the West Campus has continued to evolve, from this point, as a field of distinctive pavilions mostly bearing the names of donors.

Saarinen began work on his MIT schemes in the early 1950s. Like Aalto, he produced inversions of the principles of the Main Campus, but his were even more direct and explicit. He continued Bosworth's infinite corridor across the road—but as an open-air pathway. He reflected the mass of the Main Campus with its two domes—but reinterpreted it as a rectangular void containing two dramatic pavilions with forms derived from circles. Background buildings and a modernist version of a cloister were to bound the space, and he even daringly proposed that the cloister should bridge across Massachusetts Avenue so that Bosworth's facade would become the eastern edge. This scheme had something in common with Mies van der Rohe's earlier composition of elegantly simple, discrete forms in space at the Illinois Institute of Technology, but it substituted arcs for straight lines and curved surfaces for planes. And in some ways it was also an architectural in-joke, a play on the figure/ground diagrams that had been popularized by Gestalt psychologists, and were all the rage among urban designers of the time. But it worked anyway.

Kresge Auditorium is a triangular dome resting, with considerable structural irrationality, on three points tied together with turnbuckled cables in the basement.[19] Its form gave rise to the delightful legend that the architect had derived it by inverting and mutilating his breakfast

grapefruit. Its miracle plastic roof soon leaked, and was later replaced, at great cost, with a metal one. The nearby Chapel, with light reflected upward from a moat into a shimmering Harry Bertoia sculpture, is a gorgeously romantic example of the spatial poetry that a great architect could sometimes create within the conventions of fifties modernism. A tiny, perfectly cylindrical form, it is absolutely unlike anything else at MIT—except, maybe, the nuclear reactor. Norbert Wiener quipped: "It will put the name of the Lord on everyone's tongue, because they will look at it and say, *Oh, my god*."[20] Conservatives complained that it wasn't *their* idea of a religious building. And the hardline modernist critic Bruno Zevi found it meretricious—dismissing it as a "pseudomystical experiment" that did not solve the problem of modern religion.

Historians and critics generally received these buildings as emblems of a problematic moment in the evolution of modernism. Within ongoing postwar debates about architecture's future, Saarinen had become a prominent advocate of stylistic pluralism—an opponent of Mies van der Rohe's admonition that it was not necessary or possible to "invent a new kind of architecture every Monday morning"[21]— and he was much criticized by more mainstream modernists for this. He saw every project as an experiment, a search for new form.[22] In the case of Kresge Auditorium, the search was for a technologically innovative solution to the ancient architectural problem of the long-span vaulted space, and it was not entirely successful. Saarinen's initial vision of a soaring concrete shell touching the ground lightly at a few points was poetic, audacious, and—as it turned out—not fully realizable. By the time the engineering and design development were done, the concrete structure, as revealed by the edge beams, had become undeniably hefty. The interior had congealed into a largely opaque mass. The critic Sigfried Giedion called the completed project "earthbound," and in

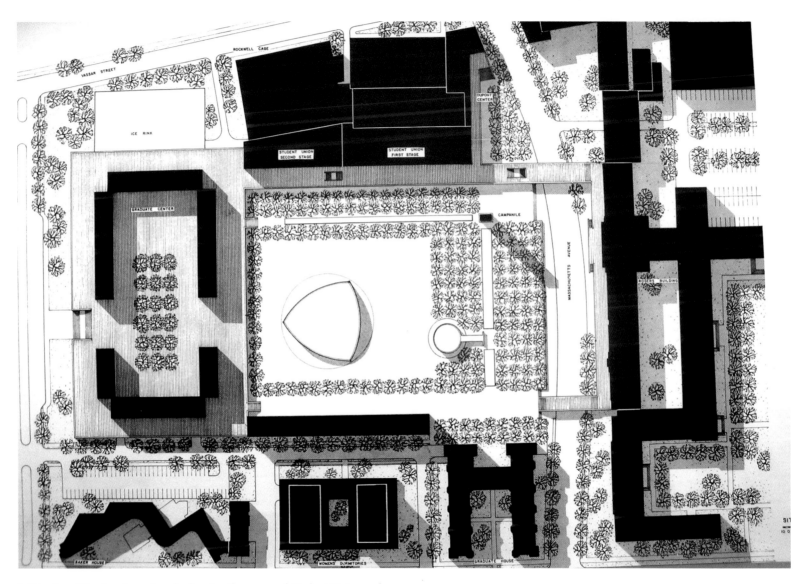

VASSAR STREET

ROCKWELL CAGE

ICE RINK

DUPONT CENTER

STUDENT UNION
SECOND STAGE

STUDENT UNION
FIRST STAGE

GRADUATE CENTER

CAMPANILE

MASSACHUSETTS AVENUE

ROGERS BUILDING

BAKER HOUSE

WOMEN'S DORMITORIES

GRADUATE HOUSE

SITE
IO O

7 Site plan of Saarinen's quadrangle showing the proposed Student Union and
Graduate Center, and the infinite corridor continued across Massachusetts Avenue
as a pathway to the athletic fields.

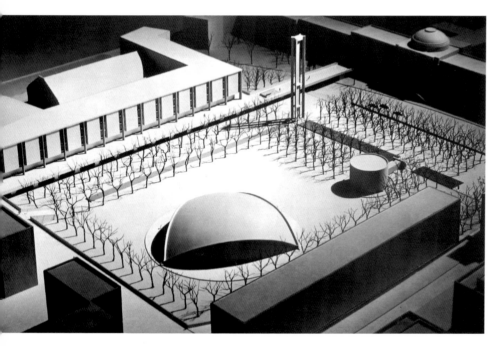

8 Model of Saarinen's proposal (one of many versions) for a modernist quadrangle confronting and contrasting with Bosworth's entry to the Main Complex at 77 Massachusetts Avenue, and incorporating a campanile and bridges across Massachusetts Avenue.

9 Kresge Auditorium under construction.

At MIT, I was not so much concerned with the dome having a relationship to the other domes. I was more concerned with what is the best possible building to place in among several, approximately five- or six-story buildings. An auditorium done as a squarish box, which can be done, would have been lower than those buildings and just did not seem to fit there. It would have blocked the space, would have just looked like a lesser cousin of the other buildings. . . . Therefore, its shape that started from the ground, went up and then returned to the ground seemed to be in better contrast with the other buildings.

–EERO SAARINEN

retrospect, Saarinen (who had an attractive capacity for reflective self-criticism) was to agree—conceding that "It looks like a half-inflated balloon."[23] But he would continue the line of structural experimentation that he had initiated at Kresge, with increasing sophistication, at Yale's Ingalls Hockey Rink, at the TWA Terminal in New York, and at Dulles Airport. And, as a judge of the architectural competition for the Sydney Opera House, he would give the young Jørn Utzon the opportunity to create the greatest curved concrete roof structure of them all.

The Chapel, by contrast, is a traditional load-bearing brick building. It alludes simultaneously to a long lineage of circular tombs, temples, and chapels, to the curves of the baroque, and to the undulating walls of Baker House. The search, here, was for a way to produce a powerful psychological effect through the theatrical introduction of natural light into a darkened interior—as it had been for Bernini in his church interiors. It was about phenomenology, not technology.

This was all far too much for Zevi, who complained that Saarinen at MIT has "chosen to dissociate form from function, construction from technological needs." He smelled mannerism. And he pointed to the awful consequences: "Mannerism did not prevent artistic creation, but was the expression of an escape from reality, of an architectural nervous breakdown. . . . Mannerist architects were unhappy and bored, so were their clients, so was their society." This was a symptom of cultural confusion and moral crisis: "They did not know what to express, and they dedicated themselves to the search for generalized forms, for shapes more astonishing than convincing." Still, he allowed: "The mistakes of great artists are always significant."[24]

By the time the modernist theorists, the iconoclastic Finns, and the cranky critics were done, there were two MITs. Just as in the city of Helsinki, there was a severe, neoclassical core with formal urban spaces confronted by a self-consciously modernist periphery of brick, concrete, glass, asymmetrical masses, light, and air. To this day, the old Main Campus and the newer West Campus face off tensely across Massachusetts Avenue. Like a middle-aged father and teenaged son, they represent the mutually irritating viewpoints and preoccupations of different generations.

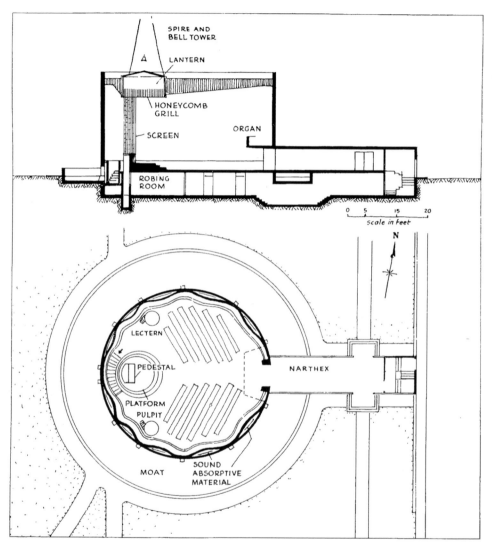

10 MIT Chapel, plan and section.

11 The Chapel nearing completion, showing its relationship to Bosworth's two domes and their rotundas.

I must say, the brick of the chapel blends in extremely well with the total picture. The chapel was really too small a building to separate itself out completely. Now it separates itself out in mass. I can ask you, would you rather have seen a square chapel? Do you think it would have gone better with the other buildings? Or should we have put fake windows to make it go with the other buildings? You see, here was a building of a different kind, different use. All the buildings that it has to go with are brick walls punctured with little windows. The chapel was a building that did not need that kind of window, so you can't relate them by knitting the surfaces together. Besides, the buildings immediately around that are no damned good and may come down. I hope so. But by doing it round, by getting the round surfaces in relation to the square surfaces, sort of separated out, by material being the same, but only more forceful in the chapel, by being round and by being the stronger texture of brick, I think it goes very well there.

—EERO SAARINEN

The first impression I had of MIT was in November 1973. I was West Coast grown, and I decided the first place I wanted to go when I came East was MIT because I wanted to see Baker House and I wanted to see Kresge Auditorium and the Chapel; they were my idea of what was going on in architecture. . . . I will never forget the real excitement of coming to MIT and going to those buildings, and being in them, and seeing how Saarinen had put a building on three points and made incredible spaces inside, and he made this chapel where the light came from below reflected from the water, and then going into Aalto's building and seeing how the corridors became lounges. I mean, he fused these two functions of buildings, and it was very exciting.

–STEVEN HOLL

12 The Chapel interior with Harry Bertoia sculpture.

13 Kresge Auditorium and the Chapel soon after completion, with industrial Cambridge in the background.

By the early 1990s there was a widespread, uneasy feeling at MIT that the formidable research and teaching machine that the campus had developed into was—much like the Tin Man—missing a heart. But what could serve for one? The usual things didn't seem to fit.

Just as the inscription "In God we trust" is the prominent centerpiece of a dollar bill, huge, landmark chapels dominate some places of learning. Cambridge has its magnificent King's College Chapel, the University of Chicago has Bertram Goodhue's Rockefeller Chapel, and the U.S. Air Force Academy in Colorado has a soaring structure in aluminum by Walter Netsch. But that would not be appropriate for MIT, which is, in general, a determinedly secular institution. Because it is a meritocracy that has always attracted talented undergraduates from migrant families, and graduate students and faculty from around the world, its community embraces a wide range of religious traditions, and it also includes a good many who simply prefer to trust in things other than questionable metaphysical constructs. It ignores most religious holidays, since to celebrate a few would be discriminatory, but to apply the admirable principle of inclusiveness and celebrate them all would make it impossible to get any work done. A monumental chapel would be as out of place here as in a shopping mall. Saarinen's little nondenominational cylinder, with its modest grace and scrupulous avoidance of traditional religious symbols and iconography, feels just about right.

Other places of learning are overshadowed, in an unseemly way, by their immense football stadiums. If you locate a stadium way out on the edge of town, as at Yale, this doesn't happen. But, if you pull it into the heart of things, as at USC or Boston College, it is unavoidable.

1 Kevin Roche's Al and Barrie Zesiger Sports and Fitness Center presents a curved, reflective wall to Saarinen's quadrangle by day—acting as an elegant background building—and at night it becomes transparent to reveal the complexities of the structural framing and the varied activities within.

Harvard accomplishes one of its characteristically discreet compromises by keeping the stadium handily nearby, but on the other side of the river with the Business School.

The problem does not arise at MIT, which has no big-time football. But it does have enthusiastic, if not always highly skilled, participation by its students in a wide range of sports and fitness activities. The north side of Saarinen's quadrangle had largely been devoted to planned facilities for these and other student needs and diversions, but upon his untimely death in 1961 it was incomplete. Apparently the money was not there for further work anyway. Gradually, other architects added projects along the edge—most notably Eduardo Catalano's magnificently macho concrete Student Center, and a bland brick-box gymnasium. By the 1990s, though, it was clear that these facilities could not adequately meet the growing needs. And from an urbanistic perspective, the edge of the quadrangle still seemed like a mouth with missing teeth.

Prompted by a committee report on Student Life and Learning[25] that identified numerous problems, and seeing the financial opportunity to make a dramatic move, President Vest convinced the Corporation to go ahead with a new building that would meet some of the most urgent recreational, fitness, and social requirements, and would finally complete the line of buildings that Saarinen had imagined. The result was the Al and Barrie Zesiger Sports and Fitness Center,[26] designed by Kevin Roche in collaboration with Sasaki Associates, and occupied in September 2002.

The distinguished veteran designer Roche had, as a young architect, been an associate of Saarinen and worked on the MIT projects, so he seemed a particularly happy choice. His initial proposal featured a soaring, curved, sawtooth concrete roof that continued the Saarinen tradition of spectacular concrete structure. Sadly, this was found to be

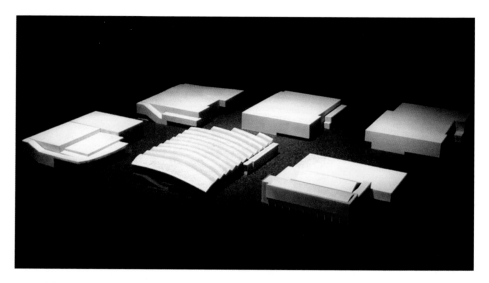

2 Models illustrating massing options.

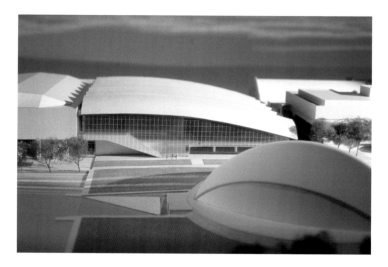

3 An initial proposal, with swooping, saw-toothed clerestory roof answering Saarinen's dome.

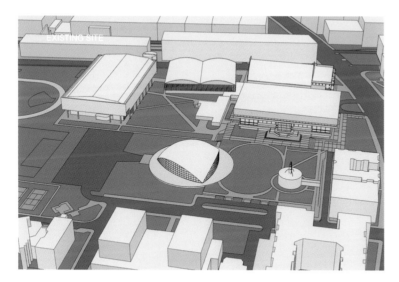
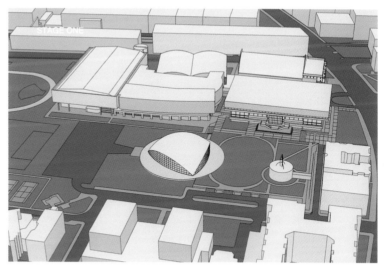

4 The urban design role of the Zesiger Center, illustrated by Roche's computer massing models, is to complete the northern edge of Saarinen's quadrangle.

Given the iconic nature of Eero's Kresge Auditorium, we decided at the outset that it would be more appropriate to design a background building rather than make too independent a statement.

–KEVIN ROCHE

beyond MIT's budget. With great restraint and finesse, he then produced a background building that presents itself to the quadrangle as a single, gently curved expanse of reflective curtain wall. With this simple gesture, it does its urban work and pays homage to the beautifully curved brick, metal, and glass of the Saarinen pavilions that it faces.

Behind the smooth casing, it is skillfully packed—like the insides of a computer—with the innumerable specialized spaces that today's sports and fitness programs demand. It has pools large and small, locker rooms male and female, squash courts, weight rooms, aerobics floors, staff offices, and many more. Owing to a tight budget, it is basically shopping mall construction, and not particularly well detailed, but it delivers what was asked for at the price the Institute's financial strategists thought it could afford. And, as shrewd and experienced architects can often do, Roche found a way to extract the possibility of one great space from the rather unpromising exigencies of the situation. He seized it to create a monumental indoor pool space that serves both athletic and social functions. As the learned old classicist Bosworth would instantly have recognized, it is MIT's Roman bath to complement its Pantheon—filled not with the likes of Diocletian, of course, but with engineers in their Speedos.

With Roche's superb piece of urban prosthetic dentistry—the insertion of a shiny, metallic tooth, like bling in a rapper's mouth, to fill an unsightly gap—the quadrangle fronting Massachusetts Avenue now presents a reasonable approximation to the geometric clarity and completeness that was projected for it back in the fifties. The space does still fade raggedly away to the west, beyond Kresge Auditorium, where Saarinen had proposed an imposing Graduate Center, and some future architect will eventually have to complete the job with a building that serves some other purpose.[27] (Urbanists have to play the long-term, strategic game, and be satisfied with what they can get in the meantime.) With its modestly but elegantly expressed athletic facility and chapel, this almost-complete ensemble of buildings and open space represents MIT's growing recognition that it must not let itself be reduced to a forcing pen for scientific and engineering talent. It raises two ambivalent cheers for body and soul.

The challenge in designing the center was to place a very complex program in a phased sequence on a difficult site and to do it in such a way as to tie together all of the existing sports spaces, encourage movement through the new complex, entice the students to participate, and finally to complete a master plan which Eero Saarinen had developed when he was designing the Kresge Auditorium and MIT Chapel. He had envisioned a continuous series of buildings along the north side of the park-like space called the Oval which would mirror the existing buildings on the south side and create an enclosed space, the centerpiece of which would be the Kresge Auditorium.
–KEVIN ROCHE

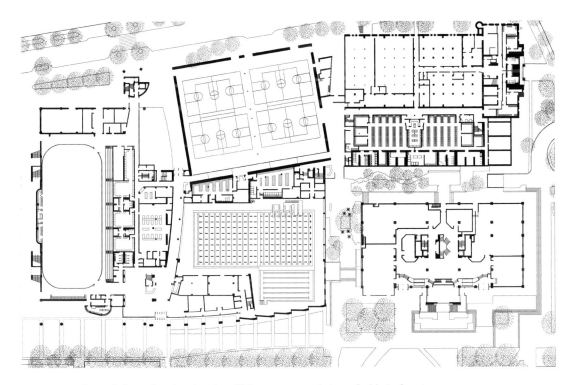

5 Ground-floor plan showing the efficient accommodation of athletic functions, circulation, and mechanical services within a tight spatial envelope.

6 The pool is the central element of the interior. Like a Roman bath, it functions as an important public space and meeting place.

7 A major cross-campus circulation route connects Saarinen's quadrangle to Vassar Street to the north, and provides views of the activity within.

8　The Zesiger Center soon after completion, showing its relationships
to Kresge Auditorium and its urban context

The facade is divided vertically into three horizontal elements. The lower section is a limestone-clad arcade as a nod to W. W. Bosworth's neoclassical academic buildings to the east across Massachusetts Avenue. The center section is a clear glass ribbon which separates the upper and lower sections. The upper portion of the façade is a glass veil over the activities inside. The structurally-glazed glass panels are fabricated of a dark grey glass and a patterned glass which eliminates direct sunlight and glare on the courts while allowing views out to the campus. At dusk the transparency becomes reversed; from the surrounding area, the interior of the building and its activities are visible resulting in a building which fulfils the Athletic Department's desire to have the athletic program at the forefront of extracurricular activities for MIT students.

—KEVIN ROCHE

The next major project of the Vest era, the Simmons Hall dormitory, had a more radical and controversial agenda. MIT had never established a collegiate residential system like its Ivy League competitors, or the closely associated but contrastingly female and bucolic Wellesley College, and had functioned mostly as an urban commuter school that relied on a subway stop, bus lines, and parking garages to connect it to the reaches of the Boston metropolitan housing market. Over the years, it had gradually added on-campus dormitory space—including, of course, Baker House—as the demand became more pressing, donors stepped up, and finances allowed. It had also relied heavily on fraternities and other small-scale independent living units scattered throughout Cambridge and the Back Bay area. As the year 2000 approached, this patchwork system was breaking down under the long-accumulating pressures on it, and the situation had reached crisis point. Simmons Hall was the centerpiece of the Vest administration's response.

The crisis had been manifested in increasingly strident dissatisfaction among faculty, staff, and students with the quality of MIT as a community, in some widely publicized binge drinking incidents, and—tragically—in some student suicides.[28] It had been diagnosed and documented—with extensive data, in the MIT way—in the same Student Life and Learning report that had prompted Zesiger.[29] With the support of his Academic Council, Vest took the decisions to strengthen counseling and other student care services, crack down on alcohol use, and begin to house all freshmen on campus. When the housing officers did their numbers, it was immediately clear that a large new dormitory would be needed to accommodate this. It also

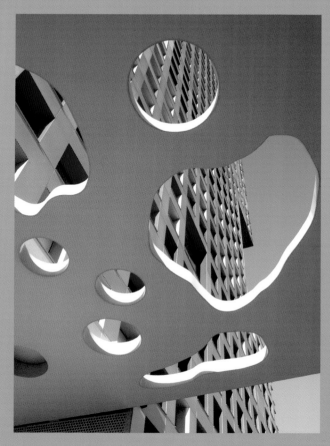

1 Simmons Hall: the interplay of grid and sponge.

2 The site for Simmons Hall—an asphalt parking lot (to the left of the green open space of Briggs Field), jammed between Vassar Street and a railroad track.

We had our first interview in November of 1998. A master plan had been completed which called for a series of very normative, pseudo-traditional buildings along Vassar Street. . . . At the interview, I explained that we would be thrilled to work at MIT, but in order to do so we would reject the master plan. Aside from its lack of consideration for its neighbors, the plan, with its call for traditional buildings and normative streetscapes, was, in our opinion, too concerned with the past. MIT is an incredible research institution, a place concerned with advancing knowledge for the sake of a better future. Why should its architecture aspire to the past? The best architecture on campus, Saarinen's Kresge Auditorium and Chapel, Aalto's Baker House, does not do this. Instead, these works celebrate the possibilities of the future. In the same spirit, we were determined to make a project that was unashamed to be part of the twenty-first century.

–STEVEN HOLL

meant that there would be a significantly reduced constituency for independent living units.

There was a squall of protest from students and alumni, since many valued—sometimes to the point of fetishization—the independent living units as refuges from the faculty-dominated rigors of on-campus life, and recalled their time spent in them as crucially formative. Some of the email was venomous. Many of the protagonists in the debate saw it as a battle for the soul of MIT. But Vest pressed on, and set an aggressive deadline for occupancy of the new dormitory at the beginning of the fall term in 2002. A founders' group was set up, and Corporation life member Dick Simmons stepped in to provide a $20 million naming gift.[30] After a much contentious debate about priorities and philosophies of dormitory design, and scrutiny of a long list of candidates from around the world, a divided architect selection committee recommended the New York architect Steven Holl for the job. It was a vote for taking the occasion as one for a serious architectural investigation—with all of the complexities, risks, and cultural responsibilities that this entails—and not just a residential space acquisition process.

The chosen site was a long and narrow one, squashed between a railway line and Vassar Street—an old industrial service street that ran along the northern edge of the West Campus's sports field—and it was just barely wide enough to serve the purpose. But selection of this site made long-term urban design sense, since the area was industrial land in transition, and MIT had been buying up parcels along Vassar for years in anticipation of eventually creating a new residential neighborhood. Building Simmons presented the opportunity to initiate development of a residential edge along Vassar, just as building Baker half a century before had initiated development of a residential edge along Memorial Drive. Eventually, two lines of residences would face each

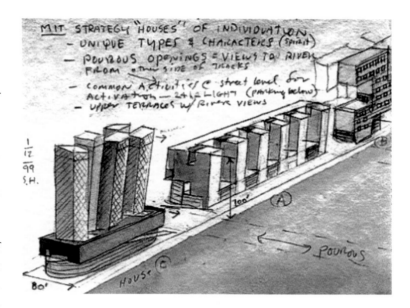

3 Massing concepts in sketch and model. Alternative schemes, lined up along Vassar Street, with Baker House and other river dormitories in the foreground, suggest the creation of an urban facade along Vassar Street and the eventual transformation of Briggs Field into a sporting quadrangle.

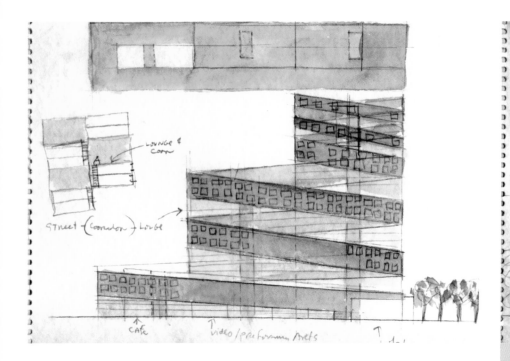

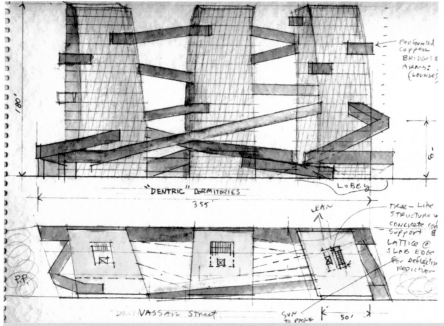

Instead of a homogeneous brick urban wall we envision the new residential strip as a porous membrane made up of four or five experimental buildings. Each of the residences would be a unique "house" with a particular identity. The visual space, light, materiality, transparency of these buildings are particularly important as they have a position free of the normal city fabric on both sides. In a sense they form a "facade" for the residential district to be built to the north of them. As a facade they must attempt to not block views. They should be "permeable."

–STEVEN HOLL

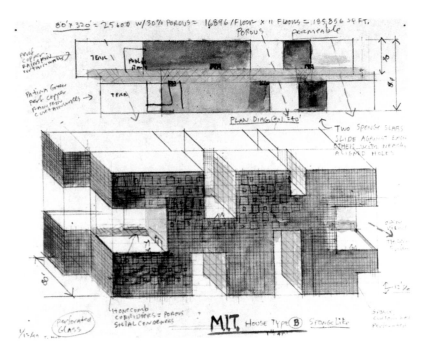

80'x 320' = 25600 w/30% POROUS = 16896/FLOOR × 11 FLOORS = 185,856 SQ FT.

PLAN DIAG(RAM) ±40'

M.I.T. House Type B Spongelite

4 Notebook sketches of alternative schemes.

other across the wide, green expanse of the playing fields, form a great new quadrangle, and complete the spatial definition of the West Campus. But that was a long way off, and meanwhile, the isolation and geometric constraints of the site posed some tough architectural challenges. Furthermore, the city of Cambridge had imposed stringent height limits, and the politically active Cambridgeport community to the north was vociferous in its demands to have a say in what was done.

There was a tradeoff. This strategy entailed some costs and complexities that could have been avoided on an easier site, but it returned MIT to a tradition of building with larger, longer-term urban goals in mind. Bosworth had a clear and compelling conception, within a Beaux-Arts framework, of the relationship of buildings and landscape to form an overall campus composition. Eero Saarinen pursued a similarly integrated approach in his modernist quadrangle. In both cases, though, the proposed landscape designs were only partially executed, and the siting of MIT buildings, over the decades, has often been highly opportunistic. It has responded to the emerging availability of potential construction sites as the Institute has acquired plots of land on its periphery, to the convenient availability of access and utilities, and to the ability of politically adept deans and department heads to claim desirable real estate for their projects. As a result, the campus fails to take full advantage of its spectacular riverfront, and many of its outdoor spaces are just leftover patches of ground with a desultory overlay of ornamental horticulture and lawn trees. The selection of the Simmons Hall site was an act of will aimed at reversing this.

Acutely aware of the difficulties he faced, conscious of his role as a standard-bearer of the architectural avant-garde, and with an eye on Aalto's great precedent across the field, Holl began a series of explorations of radical new dormitory forms. Some of them produced bug-eyed bewilderment among those at MIT who were still struggling to

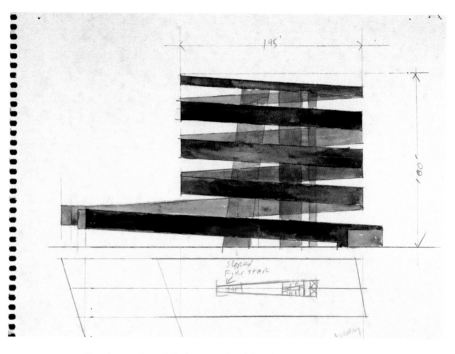

5 Sketches and model photograph of the "folded street" option that was initially favored, and developed in detail, before being rejected by MIT as too difficult and risky.

At the time, we felt that the folded street was the strongest of the four ideas. . . . Things were going very well and everyone was very excited about the scheme, but there was a problem. The as-of-right building code specified a one-hundred-foot maximum height along Vassar Street. At the outset of the project, we were assured that MIT would secure a variance for our 180-foot scheme. However, after four months of design development work, we were given an ultimatum. MIT would not pursue the variance, so we would have to revise the scheme to fall within the height restriction. . . . We could start over, or we could resign.
–STEVEN HOLL

come to terms with Aalto, and some foundered owing to Cambridge City Council or floor space efficiency issues. Eventually, Holl and the client group settled on a scheme grounded in the metaphor of a porous sponge that would clearly define the Vassar Street edge but not read as a looming, impermeable wall or obstruct access to the Charles River area from the Cambridgeport residential neighborhood. It would also, they hoped, be sufficiently dramatic to establish the direction in which its neighborhood was moving, signal to incoming students that they were held by the institution to be special and important, and set up some principles for further residential development along the street. It picked up some visual references from the industrial forms and materials that had long characterized its gritty neighborhood, but it had no hint of Georgian or Collegiate Gothic, and there was nowhere for ivy to grow.[31] Nearby Cambridge residents expressed concern about dazzling sunlight reflecting off its bright metal surfaces, but they needn't have worried; they lived on the north side of the building.

Simmons was not quite complete, but it was far enough along to receive a certificate of occupancy in time to receive students seeking housing in September 2002. Holl's spectacular design was published throughout the world. It was extensively and enthusiastically reviewed in the architectural and popular press, and received every imaginable architectural award. But those who had fiercely rejected the very idea of housing all freshmen on campus, and occupants who resented the swarms of architectural tourists with cameras, were not so sure. Outraged traditionalists (as outraged traditionalists usually do) enumerated their Rorschach projections onto it: "computer chip standing on edge," "a sort of concrete womb nightmare," "the dungeon that the Count of Monte Cristo was left to rot in."[32] From the popular children's cartoon character, it acquired the irreverent nickname Spongebob Squarepants.

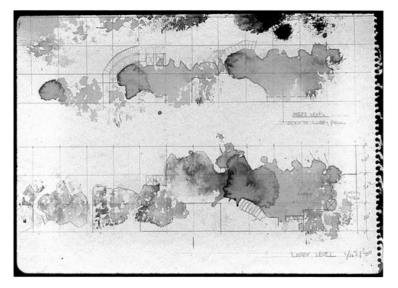

We develop techniques to execute each concept. In this case, sponge painting and ruled surfaces propel the ideas forward. . . . At the beginning, I went out and bought a bunch of sea sponges. Sea sponges have a very complex, organic structure that exhibits an incredible variety of spaces. . . . I laid out the rectangle of the building footprint on my drawing table and made a series of ink drawings with the sponges— just smashing the sponge onto the page. Then I had to go to Europe. While I was gone, people in the office took those drawings and connected the different floor plans with ruled surfaces.

—STEVEN HOLL

6 Development of the sponge concept, from watercolor painting to inhabited reality.

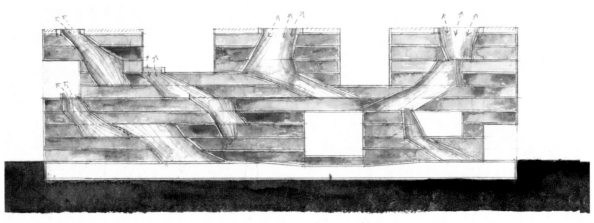

Certain more conservative critics hate the voids, referring to them as "smoke signals" or "gray goo." But the response from the students has been completely different. They live in these spaces, and get to experience the way the building reveals itself.

–STEVEN HOLL

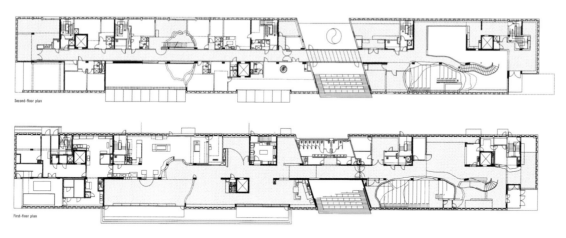

Second-floor plan

First-floor plan

7 Double-loaded corridor floor plan, showing intrusions of spongelike forms
into the regular grid.

8 Student rooms with plywood furniture.

9 Computer rendering of the main lobby and staircase.

The innovation of Simmons is not in its basic floor plan. This takes the form of a thoroughly traditional double-loaded corridor. The student room layouts and space standards are those of current, generally accepted good practice. If you look at a typical floor plan, there is not much that is unusual—apart from occasional bloblike shapes that appear to have dropped onto it randomly. The gridded external skin, though, is a unique and beautiful thing that breaks with the conventions of both the punched window opening and the glass curtain wall, does wonders with light and color, and creates some startlingly effective ambiguities of scale. The huge transverse openings that cut right through the building produce the sought-after sense of porosity at an urban scale. And, in section, open, free-form curved shapes snake up through the building, recalling the tension of grid and curve that Aalto had set up at Baker House. Robert Campbell, in the *Boston Globe,* christened them "smoke puffs."[33]

These rising smoke signals serve multiple functions. They provide a variety of unexpected vertical circulation paths, helping to break down the social barriers that typically exist between dormitory floors. They create community by associating social space with circulation, as Aalto had done with his lounges on the stairways at Baker. With their varied shapes and scales, they provide relief from the rigorously standardized, carefully calculated repetition and uniformity of the student rooms. They provide workspace, with whiteboards that can be used for group work on problems, and plenty of nooks and crannies where students can hide away with their wireless laptops. And they are simply and inexpensively built, just as ruled surfaces framed with standard metal studs and faced with plaster.

Like MIT's science-based undergraduate curriculum, Simmons Hall is uncompromisingly challenging. It stands in an industrial landscape beside a railroad track. It disdains the familiar, comforting imagery

10 Gridded concrete exterior: model and construction photograph.

of the traditional college campus. It uses materials in surprising contexts, disrupts expectations about the organization of interior space, and creates disconcerting ambiguities of scale. It demands serious intellectual engagement rather than facile response based on preconceptions. Instead of simply responding to a market, it insists on confronting its inhabitants with questions about how to break the bonds of home life and high school and learn to live in an intense intellectual community. It proposes that old houses converted into fraternities, or close approximations to mid-range motels, aren't the only answers.

The breakthrough of Simmons Hall is that, because the thickness of the floors is exactly the thickness of the structure, everything is equal. There is no way of telling how many floors there are. Suddenly, that does something. It does something in relation to other buildings around it. It does something in relation to the history of architecture. It becomes without scale.

–STEVEN HOLL

There is no color on the outside of the building; there is no color on the inside. It is only in the thickness of the wall that you find the color, in the no-man's land between inside and outside. But the color reflects into the rooms, so there is a wash of the colors within. That is what I wanted to achieve.

–STEVEN HOLL

11 Exterior details, showing deep reveals, aluminum facing, and operable windows.

Simmons did end up costing more than had initially been budgeted—mainly owing to difficulties encountered with the precast concrete construction, which is not a common technique in the United States, and with meeting the aggressive schedule. This both reduced the funding available for future products and hurt the cause of adventurous architecture and campus design at MIT. Partly as a result, the Institute's subsequent dormitories have been bereft of interesting ideas, architecturally nondescript, and tucked away in Cambridge back streets where they do little to shape the campus or strengthen its sense of community. But in a few years, the controversies will be forgotten and an extraordinary architectural achievement will remain. It will continue to represent a passion for invention, a reproach to the practice of treating dormitory space as a standardized commodity that is planned by technicians with spreadsheets and ordered up like office supplies, and a refusal to reduce architecture to historicist branding that evokes some supposedly golden era of the past. Most unforgettably, it is a celebration of the sheer joy that can be had from light bouncing seductively off beautifully crafted surfaces.

12 Digital time-bracketing images by Guy Hoffman showing light transitions across Simmons Hall over the course of several hours.

With the Ray and Maria Stata Center, MIT engaged the task of reinventing laboratory space for the twenty-first century. The need arose from the growth to prominence of a research area—information science and technology—that had not even been imagined when the campus was initially planned, and so had always lacked a suitable and permanent home. The IT boom of the nineties intensified the problem as the space demands of the various laboratories and departments in the area grew, but it also presented the opportunity to solve it by constructing an ambitious new building.

It was not that MIT had the necessary funding in the bank—far from it, in fact. But three major donors, all of whom owed their success to information technology in its various forms, promised large enough gifts to give the project credibility. The benefactors were Ray Stata of Analog Devices, Bill Gates of Microsoft, and Alex Dreyfoos, who had made a fortune from photographic technology and television broadcasting. It was a risk, but the project got the Corporation's go-ahead while fundraising continued. If ever there was a moment for betting boldly on the future of bits and electronics, this surely had to be it.

As the project evolved, its program snowballed—a process that continued right up until the addition of two levels of underground parking at the end of the design development phase. It had initially been conceived as a straightforward laboratory and faculty office building, but the realization that MIT needed to pay more attention to social space began to take hold while the project was actively under way, and this produced additions to the program. Furthermore, there was a process much like that of tacking amendments onto a bill passing through Congress. As the project gathered momentum, deans, provosts, and others realized that it

The Stata Center is a collage; I could go around Cambridge and show you a precedent for everything in it. We don't think of buildings as individual buildings; if you look around, you will see that they're really pieces of buildings collaged together. In fact, you usually don't see whole buildings—that's what creates a kind of urbanism, and I'm just continuing that.

–FRANK GEHRY

1 The Stata Center: a complex, nonrepetitive building that presents many different faces to its highly varied surroundings.

would provide their best opportunity to get various things that were important to them done, so they maneuvered to get elements added to the program. The result was a successively expanding scope and budget, and addition of complexity to the management and design tasks.

Conventional management wisdom might suggest that all this should have been much more tightly disciplined. In fact, though, the project team managed to deal with the growing and changing demands, and the eventual result was a project that responded much more completely and sensitively to the MIT community's needs, and was socially and architecturally far richer than it otherwise would have been. Large and complex building projects that evolve over several years, in dynamic and unpredictable environments, present a choice between rigid stabilization of the parameters at the expense of responsiveness, or responsiveness at the cost of increased process complexity. It was not necessarily premeditated, but MIT wisely (at least in retrospect) chose the latter.

Selection of the architect was a lengthy and contentious process, since all of the many stakeholders in the project realized that the choice would strongly determine the character of the eventual result—and they did not all have the same priorities. There was a broadly representative selection committee, and it did its homework. It first compiled a long list, with suggestions from a wide range of sources, and collected examples of the work of listed architects. After much debate, it reduced this to a short list of six—carefully selected to represent, in the best possible way, a range of very different attitudes and approaches. Buildings were visited, references were sought, and the six were extensively interviewed. Following further debate, it came down to two distinguished but very different architects. After listening to the committee, his architectural advisor, and his executive vice president, President Vest made the final choice of Frank Gehry.

2 The site at the corner of Main Street and Vassar Street (center) before demolition of Building 20 and the parking garage.

I'm a faith-based practitioner. I assume that, if I ask enough questions when I'm engaged with a project, and if I'm dealing with people who are thinking about their environment—what they want and what they need—then I will come away with a roadmap or a path to which to respond. I don't come to the table with a preconception. . . . You take things as they are given to you, respond and work on them, with the knowledge you bring to the table.

I was raised on Talmudic discussions with my grandfather—it's all about questioning and "Why?" You make a statement and then he makes a counter-statement—it's a constant inquiry, and it seems totally irrelevant while you're doing it, but it hones your thinking and sooner or later you come up with an essence. And everything comes back, in some way, to the golden rule.

That's what I believe I'm doing with my buildings—following the golden rule. I want to be a good neighbor. I respect the other architects whose work surrounds mine. Some of it I like, some of it I don't. But there is a growing model of urbanism in America, in the world—and I optimistically believe that this has something to do with democracy—there's a pluralism and a collision of ideas, something almost Talmudic. And that collision of ideas is the process by which you come to conclusions yourself. You make your statement, and you hope that it has positive effects.

—FRANK GEHRY

The attraction of Gehry was not that he had recently gained rock-star fame with his Bilbao Guggenheim, although this did have the effect of clouding the discussion with animadversions—pro, con, often resignedly ironic, sometimes enviously snide—on the culture of celebrity, the role of iconic buildings on university campuses, and the deplorable nouveau-riche desire for trophy buildings. It was his refusal to take anything for granted, his capacity to ask searching and fundamental questions, his obvious ability to translate subtle and complex intentions into sophisticated spatial and material responses, and his track record of many decades of adventurously innovative building under conditions of tight budgets, demanding programs, and complex site conditions. He had proudly shown the selection committee his early project for the Rouse Company headquarters, and some projects in gritty Los Angeles contexts, to illustrate the problem-solving approach that he would take.

And so it proved to be. Gehry engaged the community of future inhabitants in wide-ranging, detailed discussions to ferret out not only their formal space needs and technical requirements, but also the characters and ideals of their research and learning cultures, and their aspirations for the future. His team produced dozens of models to embody propositions and structure critical discussion of them, and he interjected unexpected metaphors to shake up preconceptions—on one occasion provoking uproar by suggesting the model of an orangutan village. Using the classically modernist methodology in which he had been trained, he produced a kit of rectangular, color-coded wooden blocks to represent required functional volumes, and then assembled these into alternative massing models that satisfied adjacency requirements and site constraints. Gradually, as a consensus on the functional diagram and basic massing stabilized, he began to make fluid sketches and to sculpt the form with shaped wooden blocks, cardboard, and

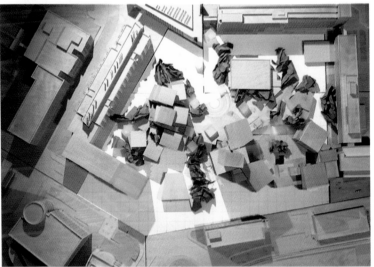

3 Program massing model and proposed master plan for the Stata Center, the associated quadrangle, and the Vassar and Main Street frontages.

4 Explorations of overall form developed, at the schematic design stage, through quickly constructed models using varied materials.

5 Sketches developed in parallel with models.

crumpled paper. As he moved the project into design development and construction documentation, he and his partner Jim Glymph transferred the evolving model from physical format into a three-dimensional digital model maintained by the Catia system. They used this model for collaboration on construction issues with fabricators and the general contractor, and eventually as the definitive source of construction information.[34] Ground was broken in March 2000, and the complex opened in May 2004.

The chosen site was that of the beloved and much-mythologized but worn-out Building 20 on Vassar Street—a choice that was rationally opportunistic in terms of land availability and use and functionally appropriate in terms of its proximity to related campus activities. (The Stata Center was to be Building 32—a hexadecimal allusion to the numerical label of its predecessor.) Furthermore, it was appealing to imagine a new building rising, phoenixlike, from the place where much of today's MIT culture of electrical engineering and computer science had been formed. Gehry's building responds to this site by continuing and completing the long line of laboratory buildings along Vassar Street, creating a major new campus entrance to the northeast (a traditionally industrial and blue-collar area on which the campus had hitherto turned its back), and forming the third side—along with two existing laboratory slabs—of an emerging new campus quadrangle. Eventually, all going well (again, urbanists must play the long-term game, and have faith), the fourth side of the quadrangle will be closed by yet another laboratory building along Main Street, the surface car parking lot that remains will be removed from the interior, and it will be greened according to a plan that has been developed by the landscape architect Laurie Olin.

Parking, as usual, was a headache.[35] It is mostly accommodated underground, which was not the original intention. MIT had long planned for a major parking structure across Vassar Street from the Stata site, and the Cambridge architect Harry Ellenzweig had completed an exceptionally elegant design for it. But MIT's building committee gradually began to realize that this structure would block effective expansion of the campus to the north, and eventually canceled the project just before it was scheduled to begin construction. Because the design of Stata was almost complete at this point, and it would be enormously costly and disruptive to the schedule to embark on a major reworking, Gehry decided to keep the design mostly unchanged and simply introduce an enormous transfer slab at ground level, over the excavation, to accommodate the necessary difference between the structural system above grade and that below. But this late change of direction also created an architectural and social opportunity, which he enthusiastically exploited; the entrance to the underground parking draws pedestrians through Stata's public spaces, enlivening them and creating numerous opportunities for chance encounters.

At the ground-floor level, the building continues the infinite corridor system to integrate it into the interconnected monolith of the Main Complex. The basement tunnel system, and some upper-floor corridors, link up as well. But the circulation system and its role have been critically rethought and transformed. Instead of a straight, narrow, interior corridor flanked by anonymous doors that offers little invitation to linger, few opportunities for encounter and social interaction, and no natural light, it is broad and generous. It has numerous nooks and crannies, with seating, that can be appropriated for conversation or as informal workplaces, together with blackboards to write on. Like a good street, it is lined on either side with social uses and attractors of activity—information desk, elevators and stairs to the upper floors, cafeteria with tables that create a sidewalk café atmosphere, major

6 Some of the many models used to explore functional organization, interior space, and exterior massing.

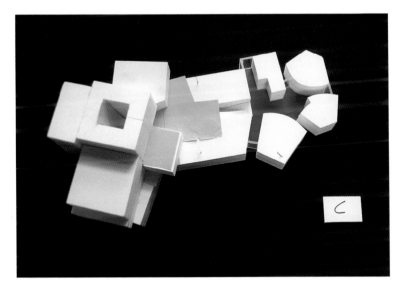

Before they hired me, I predicted they'd all want what they had, and that's exactly what they said at the first meeting. They said, "How do you break out of what we're used to?" We said, "Well, you try things; you start things." They said, "Like how?" So that's when we said, "Let's try a number of ways to organize the staff offices and the shared spaces." And we did, and got them involved.

–FRANK GEHRY

They loved Building 20 because they could beat it up. It wasn't precious, so that's why I started saying, well, look, the real issue here is how do you make a Building 20–like environment where you feel comfortable banging the walls out, putting up stuff, doing things, but it's up to date and it solves the main problem. The main problem that I was given was that there are seven separate departments that never talk to each other. And when they talk to each other, if they get together, they synergize and make things and it's gangbusters. . . . So they asked me to make places where people could bump into each other, so we made these two C-shaped buildings and in the bottom put the street and the communal stuff and created a little village.

—FRANK GEHRY

auditoriums, classrooms, health club facilities, a child-care center, and an exhibit of evocative souvenirs from Building 20. The section is organized to bring daylight in at various points, and to animate the interiors as the light changes—a stark contrast to the fluorescently lit corridors of much of Bosworth's building, and even more drearily of its successors.

On the upper floors, it consists mostly of laboratory space and faculty offices. The vast square footage of this use is organized in several layers of large-footprint "warehouse" space, and then the building mass differentiates into two towers as it rises. Why two towers? Well, a reality of large university buildings today—those, at least, that are not totally funded by some government agency—is that they must be articulated into what the fundraisers call "naming opportunities" to recognize the various donors. So there is a Gates Tower to the east and a Dreyfoos Tower to the west. This bifurcation makes little sense functionally, as everyone concerned with the project realized, but it was essential to getting the project funded and done.

Since research directions are unpredictable, and since it is increasingly clear that many of the most exciting developments occur at the boundaries and unexpected intersections of established fields, the laboratory space is organized for long-term flexibility and to maximize the opportunities for interactions among research groups. Partly, this is accomplished through choice of systems; the building has a raised floor for distribution of services and displacement ventilation (which, incidentally, makes the building energy-efficient), and the partition system is designed for easy reconfiguration. Partly it is done through transparency; there is extensive use of glass, plus an organization in plan and section that provides endless vistas through the building to make the ongoing work visible. Partly it is a matter of spatial arrangement; the research groups are mostly housed in interlocking, three-

The offices, the little sanctuaries, the hallowed places that these guys really want, they're on the periphery so they become like the walls of the building. The whole perimeter is offices and they face in various ways, interrupted occasionally with breaks of glass that look out on the campus—those are the small break areas.

—FRANK GEHRY

7 The final scale model.

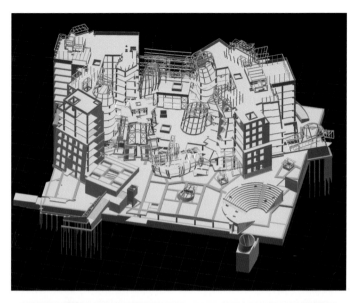

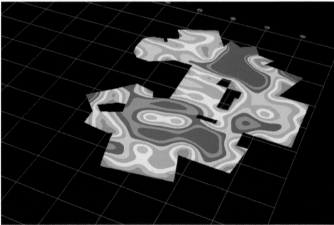

8 Structural modeling using Catia: overall model and floor slab deflection.

We've been using software from the aircraft industry, Catia—and for quite a number of years. We bumped into it quite accidentally, because I started using curves that were hard to represent to the construction industry. We needed to demystify it so that they could bid on it in a rational way. . . .

Everyone's had the experience of a building that comes in over by something, and then the contractor will say to the owner: "Hey, if you straighten that curve, I'll save you a million bucks." The owner, who doesn't have the spare million, is going to say yes. And the architect becomes marginalized in a split second.

The client doesn't *want* you to be marginalized—they want you to deliver what you have—but it's intangible to them. The computer changes the game by creating such a precise definition of the parts and pieces that the contractors are actually quite happy. Instead of looking at something that doesn't look like anything they've ever done, and just doubling the bid, they take it seriously, and spend time in the early stages, and develop a fairly precise cost response. That lets the architect take more responsibility, which makes him a better partner. . . . And, the more you can become that, the more likely you're going to achieve everyone's goals.

–FRANK GEHRY

dimensional pinwheels of space that have clear centers to provide identity and places to come together, but ambiguous boundaries that can shift as required. And partly it is attitude; the materials, finishes, and interior systems are not precious and unchangeable, but—like those of Building 20—invite modification and reconfiguration by the occupants over time.

On the exterior, Stata presents a relatively straightforward facade to Vassar Street, with entrances at either end, and forms a roughly C-shaped mass on the southern, sunny, quadrangle side. Stepping up into the interior of the C are staggered, landscape terraces to create some welcome artificial topography on MIT's otherwise dead-flat campus. The upper levels are raised into the sunlight and protected from the wind so as to create a warm microclimate in which spring begins a little early and fall comes late. Olin's landscaping, as it steps up the terraces, presents in miniature the various ecosystems of Massachusetts—from low wetlands to mountaintops. The overall composition can be read as a radical reinterpretation of the traditional European college quadrangle, with its formal face to the street contrasting with a green, more private interior.

The external surfaces are highly reticulated, there are canyonlike spaces slashed through the interior, and the windows are operable so that—despite the building's large footprint—few of its inhabitants are denied natural light, view, and ventilation. In addition, discrete, figural forms perch on the major masses, like the houses of a mountainside village, or—as I suppose Bosworth would see it—the theaters, shrines, and temples of a classical acropolis. As they foreshorten in the distance, they begin to recall the cubist canvases of Fernand Léger. They house elements of particular public and social importance: seminar and meeting rooms, a particularly prominent robotics lab, and a bar. They are Gehry's means of breaking down and humanizing the scale of

It's a theater and it's accessible. It faces south, so in winter it will get some sun. . . . It creates a climate that's 300 miles south of Cambridge, so maybe someday there'll be cherry blossoms from Washington.
–FRANK GEHRY

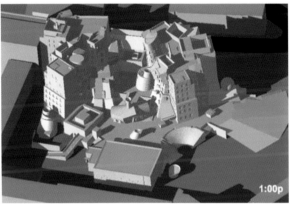

9 Shadow studies of the exteriors spaces produced from the digital model.

10 Structural models and corresponding
construction work.

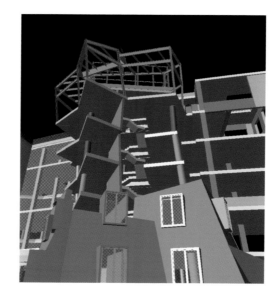

what would otherwise be an overbearing mass, and they provide him an opportunity to create a collage of colors, materials, and shapes that respond to elements in the surrounding urban context. Part of the fun of the building is in deciphering these allusions. Or, if all this offends your sense of what a sensible building should be, you can let loose and riff on earthquakes, piles of squashed beer cans, and Toontown.

Buildings, like software, always need some debugging, and Stata began this process in 2004 when the first users took possession. Like any building with a lot of glazing details, it sprang a few leaks in the first major rainstorm—but these were easily found and fixed, since critics of the building gleefully pointed them out. Sound-absorbing finishes had been value-engineered out in some areas, and this proved to be a bad idea—probably meaning that they will eventually, in piecemeal and expensive fashion, be put back in. As a protest against what some thought was excessive internal transparency, paper went up on a few glass walls—in one case, with self-deprecating wit, posters of orangutans—but most of it soon came down again. Some of the bug reports went to the project manager's punch list, but most bugs, as intended, were worked out by the users themselves as—learning to take advantage of the interior's built-in flexibility—they made it their own and adapted it to their specific needs. After a couple of years, it was clear that the building's long-term evolution would more closely resemble that of an open source project than Microsoft Windows.

Stata has turned out to provide a challenging and intellectually sophisticated environment that takes strong positions on several much-debated issues of current architecture and campus design. In its nonrepetitive, highly articulated and particularized forms, it challenges the industrial-era orthodoxy that laboratory and office space should become a standardized, modular commodity that organizations like universities accumulate in their space inventories and allocate through

11 Digital modeling and erection of CAD/CAM-fabricated metal skin.

12 Ground-floor plan showing the Student Street and accompanying
public functions.

13 The Student Street.

As we worked on the plans we were asked to include materials handling for that whole part of the campus, and it had to be cheap. So I came up with the idea of building it on grade and creating a terrace that raised the level of the courtyard, Compton Court, and I got really happy with that. Now, as luck would have it, the materials handling ended up going in the basement, so I didn't have any reason for it any more. But the client group discovered that they needed more space, which they thought they could afford, so they came up with a program of classrooms on the ground level. By doing so we retained the terrace and we were able to make the Student Street—it's an extension of the Infinite Corridor, and it shows a way of doing that without just a straight line. It has spaces for students to stop and tables where people can sell things—they can sell their fellow students ideas.

–FRANK GEHRY

The interiors are not finished or even finite; it's a very open-ended system. The idea is that the rugged individualists who are inhabiting the building are going to intervene; they're going to bring in their stuff. They already have, and over time this building will change and become theirs. I believe it's strong enough to survive that, but we'll see.

–FRANK GEHRY

14 Sixth-floor plan showing interiors of laboratory towers.

15 Laboratory space interior.

bureaucratic processes. It stands, instead, for the importance of place and identity. It also resists the subtle and attractive position that has been compellingly articulated by Robert Venturi over the years—that work space of all kinds should be simple, modest, and unostentatious rather than twisted into dramatic forms, and that the iconography of a building should instead be carried inexpensively by facades and signs. To this, Stata opposes the arguments that large footprints and masses require articulation to humanize the scale and infiltrate daylight, views, and air; people who inhabit a building for a long time come to value variety and animation; and the use of computer technology in design, fabrication, and on-site operations now allows complex, nonrepetitive buildings to be produced within normal budget and schedule constraints.

It also questions some unexamined dogmas of technical rationality, and reminds us that good engineering depends on getting the metrics right. To an eye accustomed to the low-ceilinged, fluorescently lit laboratory spaces of the past, the soaring spaces of Stata can seem absurdly wasteful. But Gehry knew that volume is quite cheap and could enable him to achieve many important goals. To a manager accustomed to computing the net-to-gross ratios of buildings, and strictly limiting them by standards derived from other buildings, the generous circulation spaces and unassigned nooks and crannies of Stata cry out for cutting back. But there is nothing so unproductive as a locked and empty private office, even though it looks good on the net-to-gross, whereas unassigned public spaces become highly productive when students and faculty have wireless portable devices that allow them to work anywhere, and when encouraging serendipitous encounters and group work are crucial priorities. If your goal is simply to minimize construction and operating costs, then you will also want to minimize surface-to-volume ratio, and you will end up with

MIT. State Center with its New England landscape.

16 Landscape setting designed by Laurie Olin.

a building that approximates a cube. But if you recognize that people are your most valuable resource, and that people like daylight, fresh air, and corner offices with interesting views, then you will want instead to *maximize* surface-to-volume ratio instead—and you will get something more like Stata.

And what about the cost? Unsympathetic critics were convinced that, because it broke so many of the accepted rules and conventions, it surely *must* have been hugely expensive. They just couldn't believe otherwise. Some of Boston's newspaper columnists lazily retailed the canard, even when presented with evidence to the contrary. In fact, Gehry and his team shrewdly economized by balancing a few complex shapes and spaces with a great deal of straightforward materials and construction, by making effective use of computer technology and innovative arrangements with fabricators to gain efficiencies in design development and construction, and by making tough tradeoffs as needed to meet the budget goals that were set by the MIT managers of the project. In the end, on a dollars-per-square-foot basis, it came out to no more than the median for comparable buildings constructed in the United States at roughly the same time.[36] It simply put the money in different places, in response to the different priorities that had been elicited by the process of engaging the building's constituency and energetically developing and exploring possibilities that weren't obvious at the outset. From one perspective, that's a pretty good definition of an architect's central task.

Why is the landscape of MIT essentially in the early nineteenth century? Here we are in the beginning of the twenty-first century, with tree lawns you could find anywhere. It's not that the trees are bad—the trees are nice, the paths work. It's a workable place. But here we are in the age of the Internet, at a point where you could be anywhere and do your business with the most intellectually advanced colleagues on the planet—why should you be in a place that looks like hell? I can just see people saying, "I'd rather be in Palo Alto," and off they go.
–LAURIE OLIN

I don't think it's a perfect building. MIT isn't perfect and I'm not perfect, but what I treasure is the client relationship and the friends I've made in working on the project. The people who inhabit this building are some of the most creative scientists alive on earth.

–FRANK GEHRY

17 Digital time-bracketing images by Guy Hoffman showing light transitions across the south face of Stata over the course of several hours.

Whereas computer science is mostly grounded on silicon-based hardware, brain and cognitive science deals with carbon-based hardware—though at some level of software abstraction, one can argue, the distinction ceases to matter. So it made both practical and symbolic sense for MIT to locate its new Brain and Cognitive Sciences Complex (BCSC) directly across Vassar Street from Stata, with a bridge planned to connect the two.

Like computer science, brain and cognitive science emerged from the convergence of earlier research fields and emerging technologies—notably psychology, artificial intelligence, molecular biology, and medical imaging. It is even more recent, and by the late 1990s it was becoming superheated, with Nobel-caliber researchers willing to bet their futures on it, talented students flocking to it, and research funding agencies and benefactors eager to support it. There was a general sense among scientists in the know that first-movers and fast-movers would be rewarded with major scientific breakthroughs. Clearly it was crucial to MIT's future as a global research leader. But the relevant researchers were scattered around the campus, they needed room to expand, and they needed to be brought together as an intensely interactive intellectual community. It was time to think about a major new building that would not only meet these needs, but also make visible to science and engineering research talent, funders, and the world in general MIT's commitment to the field.

The opportunity to seize the initiative presented itself as Y2K dawned. Patrick J. McGovern—founder of the International Data Group (IDG)—and his wife Lore McGovern announced a gift to

1 The light-filled atrium of the Brain and Cognitive Sciences Complex. Photograph originally published in *House & Garden*.

One of the problems of architecture is that, as designers, we have an ability, I hope, to understand each problem individually, but we also have what you might call a grab bag of images. Like Santa Claus, you carry it on your shoulder, and every time you're in trouble you reach into it and pull out some images and slap them on the building. I think the trick is to be patient and not to bring them out too early. You have to really get into the problem and understand it, and slowly the thing begins to take form. . . . You can always impose your will, but if you do it too soon it's silly; you've missed a chance to understand what this building wanted to become, in the sense that it had so many parameters. That goes doubly, of course, when you work for a university and there isn't a central client.

–CHARLES CORREA

MIT to create the McGovern Institute for Brain Research. The carefully structured gift was expected to yield $350 million, over a twenty-year period, to support a major ongoing research program. At the announcement, Pat McGovern recalled his student days at MIT exploring neurophysiology, neural networks, and computer science. Then, in 2002, the Picower Foundation gave $50 million to create the Picower Center for Learning and Memory—with a significant proportion of the gift going toward construction. MIT's administration decided, in consultation with the donors, to go ahead with a building that would accommodate the two emerging research institutes and the existing Brain and Cognitive Sciences Department. The design and construction schedule was to be an aggressive one; the scientists and the donors wanted to get on with it.

The stakes were high. Research competition among major universities is not a genteel business. Often, the first to move effectively into important new areas gains enormous advantages. MIT saw an opportunity to get a jump of several years on its major competitors and was anxious not to blow it.

The obvious temptation, in this sort of situation, is to play it safe architecturally—to go for a straightforward, pragmatic building that satisfies the most obvious functional requirements while minimizing the risks to schedule and budget. There is a clamor for quick and predictable results, the penalties for failure are severe, and the necks of leaders and managers are clearly on the line. Unavoidably, though, a project of this magnitude, built in a sensitive urban neighborhood by an institution that takes pride in its social and cultural leadership, must also satisfy some demanding additional requirements. In particular, the BCSC project needed not only to cluster brain and cognitive scientists at one location, but also to create the conditions for an intense intellectual community—a community that would encourage connection

Wet-lab buildings are highly structured entities. Because of the critical interrelationships of the facilities they contain (offices, labs, and support facilities) their floor plans are generated by rigorous diagrams that must run consistently through the length of the building. So the architectural form becomes a kind of extruded section, with enough floors, and enough length to each floor, to generate the area the program specifies.

This is why a wet-lab building usually ends up looking rather like a loaf of bread, sawed off to match the square-footage specified in the program. Given the complex functional relationships it contains, this seems inevitable. Look around Kendall Square—there are quite a few examples of what we are talking about. And each of them is really an autonomous object, paying no attention to its neighbors, concerned only with its own internal logic. With the result that despite all the brave attempts at "urban design," Kendall Square continues to look somewhat like the bottom of the sea.

So we knew that the Brain and Cognitive Science Project had to go beyond the internal compulsions of its floor plans. It must also respond to the urban context in which it was going to be located, i.e., the neighboring streets, vistas, buildings, and so forth. Only thus could it help make Kendall Square a better place for people to live and work in. . . .

Because of the massive floor space specified in the program (450,000 sq. ft.), we had to use the whole site—right up to the triangular corner at the intersection of Main and Vassar. This meant that the orthogonal geometry of the racetrack had to somehow adjust to the peculiar shape of the plot. There are several ways to do this, including having each racetrack run parallel to the road it faces. But we found the best strategy was to keep the all the racetracks parallel to Vassar—and then step back the system as it reached Main—which runs at an angle. This created a series of large openings—"urban windows"—which create the jumps in scale we needed to articulate the long facades.

—CHARLES CORREA

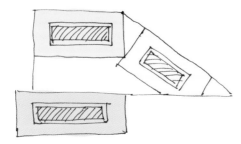

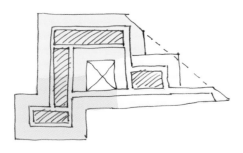

2 Sketch illustrating the adjustment of laboratory spaces, with racetrack corridors, to the irregular site.

3 Typical floor plan showing the central atrium, the three sets of racetrack-corridor laboratories clustered around it, and the large spaces that emerge at the perimeter to provide opportunities for urban windows.

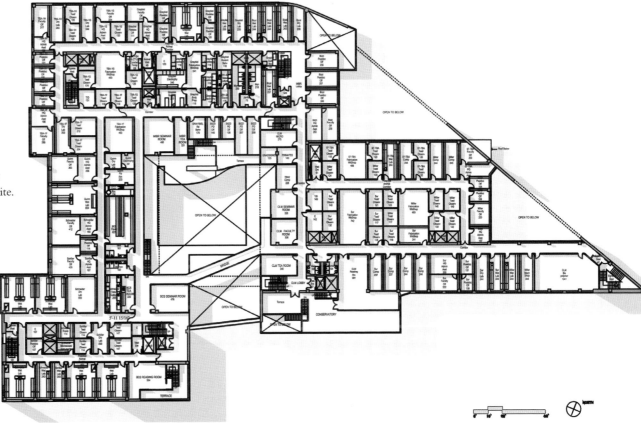

Kendall Square is really a terrible place. You've got these huge monsters, each autonomous, with its own internal logic, paying no attention to the street or to the others around it. It's a case study of what's wrong with whatever we've been doing for the last fifty or seventy years. There's no scale; it's just huge things with space around them. So, first of all, I wanted to do something that really looked as though it belonged where it is—an urban building, specific to that site.

—CHARLES CORREA

4 Elevations, study model, and completed Main Street face showing jumps in scale created by urban windows.

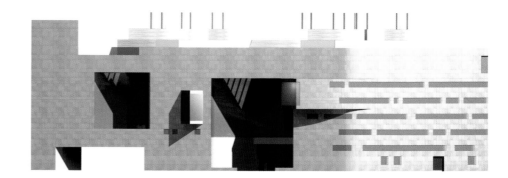

and interaction, and so maximize the value of having so much scientific talent in one place. It needed to humanize the scale of the massive building that the program demanded, and to form graceful relationships to streets on three sides and a railway line passing through the site. And it needed to respond, in some architecturally compelling way, to the powerful presence of Gehry's new building across the street. Playing it safe would not suffice; a sophisticated and imaginative architectural response would be essential.

To bring the necessary combination of capabilities to the project, MIT chose not to engage a single architecture firm, but to put together a team consisting of Goody Clancy & Associates of Boston, and Charles Correa Associates of Bombay. Goody Clancy had established a strong relationship with MIT's biologists, and had designed several successful laboratory buildings on campus. Correa had achieved worldwide renown for architectural and urban design projects such as the memorial museum at Gandhi Ashram, the Jawahar Kala Kendra

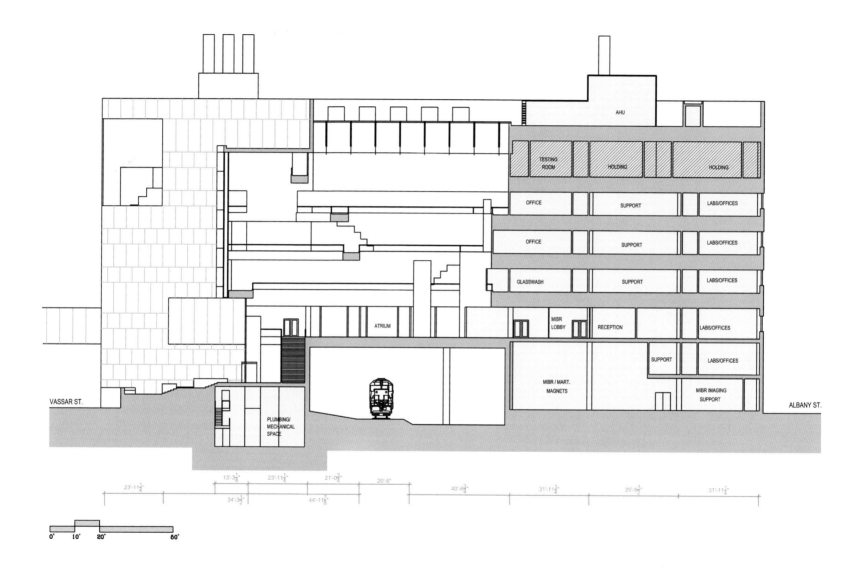

VASSAR ST.

ALBANY ST.

AHU

TESTING ROOM

HOLDING

HOLDING

OFFICE

SUPPORT

LABS/OFFICES

OFFICE

SUPPORT

LABS/OFFICES

GLASSWASH

SUPPORT

LABS/OFFICES

ATRIUM

MIBR LOBBY

RECEPTION

LABS/OFFICES

SUPPORT

LABS/OFFICES

PLUMBING/ MECHANICAL SPACE

MIBR / MART. MAGNETS

MIBR IMAGING SUPPORT

23'-11½"

13'-3¾"

23'-11¼"

21'-0¾"

20'-6"

40'-6¾"

31'-11¼"

35'-9½"

31'-11¼"

34'-3¾"

44'-11⅝"

0' 10' 20'   60'

5 Leaping the railroad: section and construction photograph.

Since bridging over the railroad is an expensive proposition, we had to restrict such leaps to as few as possible. This provided the opportunity to create a major atrium space at the center of the complex, around which are located many of the most important community facilities—such as tearooms, seminar rooms and conference rooms. This atrium leads directly down to Main Street on the other side, so that the building itself becomes a pathway, taking the MIT system over the railroad tracks and connecting it to all that new energy and enterprise which has mushroomed in the area around Main Street and beyond.

—CHARLES CORREA

Arts Center in Jaipur, and the State Assembly in Bhopal. Correa would serve as lead designer. This marriage of local and international firms was not simple to negotiate and it proved to be an uneasy one at times, but the outcome was a project that succeeded in satisfying the multiple, complex requirements.

The functional heart of the BCSC Building consists of laboratories—many of them highly serviced wet labs. These must be built to the exacting requirements of the scientists who will use them, and they allow architects little design freedom. They are highly constrained by the requirements of bench and equipment layout and service systems, and they work best when organized into large, rectangular floor plates that can be subdivided, as required, in modular fashion. They need efficient corridor circulation designed to handle laboratory staff, the flow of supplies, and laboratory animals, while providing necessary access controls. At BCSC, the laboratory floors are arranged, exactly as this logic dictates, in huge, tightly planned areas serviced by cleverly interlocking racetrack corridors.[37]

The site, however, is not a simple rectangle but an irregular parcel of land that, as a matter of accommodating the necessary square footage on a tight site and preserving street definition, demands crisp facades at the boundaries. Correa reconciled the difference between the spatial logics of the interior and the exterior in much the same way as the architects of Italian baroque churches—by letting the interior and the exterior assume the forms natural to them, and then filling the space in between with something else. In this case, though, it was not structural *poché*. Recognizing that social spaces, seminar rooms, and other such elements could fit comfortably into narrower, less regular allotments of floor space, and that they would benefit most from daylight and view, Correa pursued a strategy of pushing them (along with some very special offices) to the edges of the floor plates to take up the difference. Here they would provide opportunities for researchers from different laboratories to mix and interact with one another in more relaxed environments.

This strategy also provided the opportunity to manage the perceived scale of an otherwise massive building. It allowed Correa to create a series of large openings, which he called "urban windows," that create the scale shifts needed to articulate the long facades. He had learned the architectural lesson of the beautiful jumps in scale in Harvard's river dormitories on the other side of Cambridge, and he had applied it in a very different context in a powerful new way.

The constraints of the site and the density to which it was to be developed did not allow extension of the Main Campus pattern of quadrangles, so Correa substituted a glazed atrium—which, in any case, has obvious advantages in Boston's climate. The floor of the atrium dramatically bridges the railroad, and it rises five stories to a spectacular glass roof that reveals the dramatic exhaust stacks beyond. The building's three academic units—the Department of Brain and Cognitive Sciences, the Picower Institute, and the McGovern Institute—face onto it, so that each has a distinct identity within the whole, with the atrium space serving as a common living room at a grand scale. The south faces of the atrium and the social spaces facing onto Vassar Street are constructed from daringly detailed structural glass and provide surprising framed glimpses of Gehry's Stata facade. The walkways that surround this heart of brightness at each level serve as points of contact between the surrounding private, tightly controlled, equipment-dominated laboratory space and the public life of the campus.

On the exterior, a great flight of steps and a ramp rise up to the main entrance on Vassar Street, recalling Bosworth's steps at 77 Massachusetts Avenue. A tall, sharp prow at the acute-angled corner of Vassar and Main alludeds to I. M. Pei's concrete prow on the nearby

6 Sketches and computer graphics studies of the atrium.

Ralph Landau chemical engineering building. The exhaust stacks rise proudly on the skyline, as appropriate to a former industrial area that still features chimneystacks, a cogeneration plant, and a railroad track. Trains pass through the building and emerge, with nostalgic industrial-era drama, as from a tunnel beneath a mountain. As with Bosworth's original campus buildings, the exterior cladding is limestone—but here cast into modernist planes rather than intricately modulated classical detailing—and it is softly luminous in the sunshine.

In its massing, materials, and detailing, the whole composition acts as a discreetly sophisticated foil to Gehry's bravura performance across the street—so that the two buildings, like partners in a tango, electrify the space in between. (Gehry once remarked to me, as Correa's project took shape: "I like its body language.") They are united not by superficial similarity, but by the urban space that they define and the views of each other that they provide.

When BCSC opened, architecture critics were quick to suggest that it played the straight man—geometrically and metaphorically—to Stata. It was a suave and sophisticated Dean Martin, say, to an antic Jerry Lewis across the street. Some couldn't resist spinning the story as a morality tale of New England sobriety and rectitude versus regrettable Californian excess; Robert Campbell, in the *Boston Globe*, saw "a policeman lecturing a drunk."[38] But it is closer to the truth to say that, as good partners find ways of doing, they bring out the most interesting qualities of each other. The result is far livelier urbanism, and certainly a lot more fun, than the Tweedledum and Tweedledee that would have resulted from enforced consistency of forms and materials.

At an urban scale, the effect of the two structures is to anchor and represent an ongoing transformation of the nearby fabric of buildings and streets—one in which the large-scale workplaces of advanced science and technology incrementally replace more modestly scaled

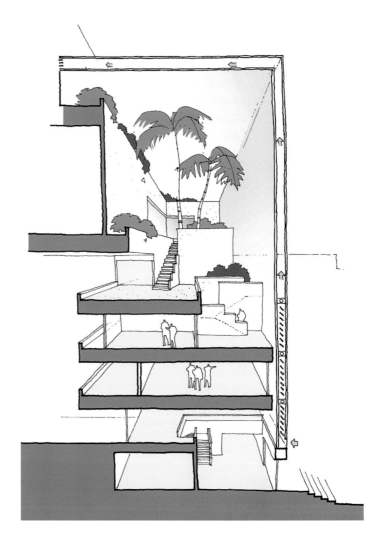

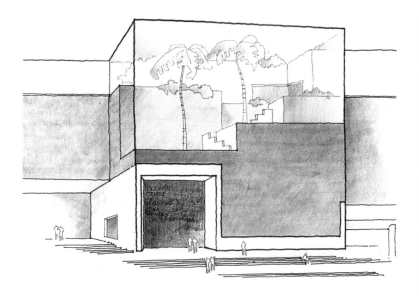

7 Conceptual sketches, computer graphics study, and photograph of the transparent indoor garden and social area above the Vassar Street entrance.

industrial construction, and former industrial service roads are converted into mixed pedestrian, bicycle, and automobile circulation routes. Stata completed the south side of Vassar Street, between Massachusetts Avenue and Main Street, in this fashion, and BCSC indicates how the north side—which, with the exception of Harry Ellenzweig's elegantly transparent cogeneration plant, consists largely of obsolete buildings and derelict lots—will someday develop in the same way. In response, MIT has remade the streetscape in between—with trees, pedestrian walkways, bicycle paths, and new street furniture—as appropriate to its new role as a major east-west campus axis.

Viewed in the context of the campus's long-term evolution, the construction of Stata and BCSC has shifted the intellectual centroid of MIT into the heart of this new geography. Under John Ripley Freeman's 1913 plan for the Cambridge campus, research activity had been concentrated on the south of the site, beside the Charles River. The exact center was occupied by steam engines, experimental coal and gas combustion, and a heat measurement laboratory, with surrounding wings devoting large areas to drafting rooms, civil and mechanical engineering, hydraulic and naval engineering, metallurgy, mining engineering, and public health. Biology got a small corner. Bosworth's slightly later plan for the Main Complex had a similar program, but the axes now crossed on a three-story-high statue of Minerva at the center of the Great Court. Eventually, fields like naval and mining engineering declined and important new disciplines like electronics and the modern life sciences emerged. In a process similar to the hollowing out of American cities as economic activity and development hived off to the edges, more up-to-date laboratory space was built on the periphery of the Main Complex, and the old core of the campus was increasingly backfilled with administrative offices, student services, and classrooms. Now, with the construction of Stata and BCSC, the mix of research

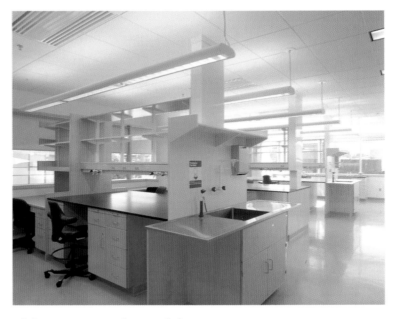

8 Laboratory space nearing completion.

A lot of the lab buildings at MIT are like rabbit warrens—fine for the rabbits who live and work there, but difficult for someone coming in. We thought if you have a corridor with one wall of a strong color, and the other of glass that leads to the outside, you'd have a pretty good idea of whether you're walking toward Main Street or toward Vassar.

–CHARLES CORREA

space uses on campus has decisively changed once more, and the focus has moved further away from the river to the northeast—to the formerly neglected backyard of the Institute at the corner of Vassar and Main.

This also represents, in vivid architectural terms, a crucial shift in the economic role of research universities. In recent decades, they have increasingly served as core components of national innovation systems, centers of high-technology industry clusters, and producers of economic growth and nearby jobs—as in the Silicon Valley area surrounding Stanford, the Route 128 area on the outskirts of Boston, and the biotechnology cluster that has more recently developed in MIT's immediate Cambridge neighborhood. The key mechanism in this is the transfer of technology from on-campus laboratories to nearby off-campus startup companies that are largely run by entrepreneurial faculty members, part-time student employees, and recent graduates. Urbanistically, the complex of new MIT laboratories defines the center of a growing high-technology neighborhood and reorients the campus to it.

It was never planned for what it became, and had no Minerva to mark it, but by 2005 a once-nondescript intersection—now surrounded by Stata, BCSC, the Whitehead Institute for molecular biology, the Broad Institute for genomics, and the cluster of biotechnology enterprises that had grown up adjacent to campus—could plausibly lay claim, at least for a while, to being the heart of the new millennium's hottest research hotspot. To understand its genetic logic, you had to look neither for an idealized representation of the subdivision of scientific and engineering effort nor for statues and symmetry, but for the varied ways in which global research and economic imperatives had encountered local exigencies in a complex, historically contingent, continually evolving urban fabric.

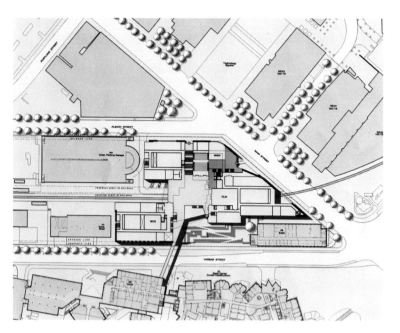

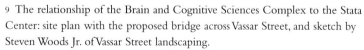

9 The relationship of the Brain and Cognitive Sciences Complex to the Stata Center: site plan with the proposed bridge across Vassar Street, and sketch by Steven Woods Jr. of Vassar Street landscaping.

10 The corner of Vassar and Main—emerging hotspot of scientific and technological innovation—viewed from BCSC.

MIT's freshman year—a long-term legacy of the postwar shift to engineering science—is notoriously tough. It force-feeds entering students with fundamental science, not only to shape some of them into future working scientists but also to provide a foundation for engineering, management, and design education. Furthermore, the Institute's great postwar expansion into a federally funded research powerhouse had been accomplished by subdividing science and engineering into increasingly fine-grained research areas that could be pursued by means of rigorous, in-depth specialization—producing a bewildering variety of narrowly focused advanced course offerings. This adds up to a clear, consistent, and mostly successful research and teaching strategy—one that has effectively differentiated the Institute from its broader-based competitors in the Ivy League and among the leading state universities—but it also has some limitations. As the 1980s dawned, MIT's president Jerome Wiesner had recognized these, and his remedy was to create a new type of intellectual enterprise—the MIT Media Laboratory.

Wiesner's idea was to create an organizational and physical setting within MIT that was not defined by traditional disciplinary boundaries, and that would provide the opportunity to bring together multidisciplinary, cross-generational teams of faculty, research scientists, and students—artists, musicians, and designers as well as scientists and engineers—to work on research projects. It would reconstitute a pattern of organization of creative work that long predated MIT's scientifically based division of labor—that of the architect or artist's atelier—and it would provide a necessary complement to the ongoing strategy of subdivision and specialization. The emphasis was to be

A sketch made in the initial stages of design has two purposes. On the one hand, it is an attempt to clearly express an intent with respect to the subject matter. On the other hand, it is an expression of the doubts and uncertainties that one entertains. One sketches not only to give expression to forms and ideas that have already been developed or that have just come to mind, but also to call forth new forms and ideas. . . . A sketch leaves things uncertain even to oneself and incorporates areas of emptiness. A sketch is appealing precisely because it records a dream that will not be fulfilled.

—FUMIHIKO MAKI

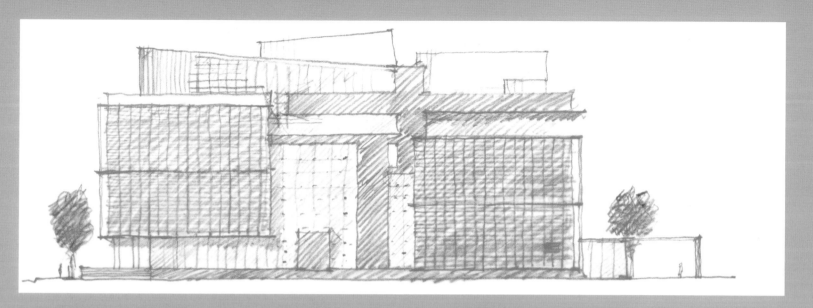

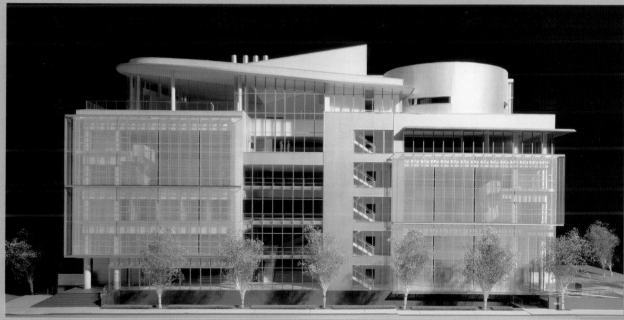

1 Sketch and model showing the Amherst Street facade of Fumihiko Maki's project for the Media Laboratory.

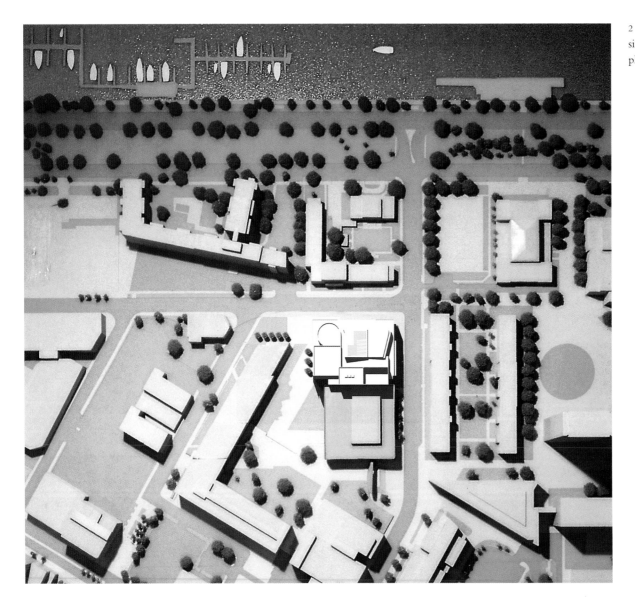

2 Site model and panoramic view of the site, with a model of the new building in place, across the Charles River.

on integration and synthesis, and learning was to take place through hands-on engagement in projects rather than formalized instruction.

The founding faculty members proudly thought of themselves as a kind of *salon des refusés* from established MIT departments and laboratories. There was the Architecture Machine Group, a successful research group that had increasingly chafed at its situation within MIT's Department of Architecture; there was a collection of graphic designers, visual artists, and musicians who had never found comfortable niches at the Institute; there were outspoken scientists from the Artificial Intelligence Laboratory; and there were electrical engineers and computer scientists who believed (a radical idea at the time) that the human interface of computer systems was the coming thing. Wiesner and the founding director Nicholas Negroponte focused the new laboratory on the emerging convergence of the computing, publishing, and broadcast industries fueled by the growing importance of digital telecommunications.[39] They would have called it the Communications Laboratory, but the School of Engineering would not let them lay claim to *that* word, so they settled for Media Laboratory. Wiesner and Negroponte were enormously successful in raising research funding and endowment (mostly from industry) to support the new enterprise, and as a result, by 1985, they were able to move it from temporary quarters into a new building.

This building, which is now known as the Wiesner Building, was designed by I. M. Pei, and it extended the group of Pei laboratory buildings that lie to the east of Bosworth's Main Complex. Owing largely to the constraints of the site, it is a free standing pavilion rather than an extension of the internally connected monolith of the Main Complex, and it does not take a linear form. Instead, it is compact and almost cubic, with white ceramic panels, rounded corners, and flush strip windows. Internally, it is organized around a central atrium with a vast and beautiful mural by Kenneth Noland. The lower floors house MIT's List Gallery and a performance space, and the upper floors organize laboratory spaces and offices around racetrack corridors. It is a characteristically cool and elegant Pei production, but it reads in the campus landscape as an impenetrable fortress (something that has added to the mystique of the Media Laboratory over the years), and there is nothing else remotely like it anywhere at MIT.

The laboratory space was originally laid out as a collection of carefully tailored zones for particular research and production activities, with meticulously worked out areas and adjacencies. But it did not stay that way for long. Technologies and research agendas rapidly changed, and the researchers repeatedly tore the space apart and reorganized it, eliminated old uses, and took over areas for new uses as short-term necessity demanded. The process was much like that of fragmentation of disk space, and the interior quickly lost any semblance of architectural coherence. Even worse, some fundamental design assumptions became obsolete; the deep, artificially ventilated and lit interior spaces had been designed on the assumption that computers occupied fixed locations and required highly controlled environments, but the emergence of robust, portable, wireless laptops with screens bright enough for use in daylight changed all that. The lesson was that detailed programs of architectural requirements—based on the immediate needs of

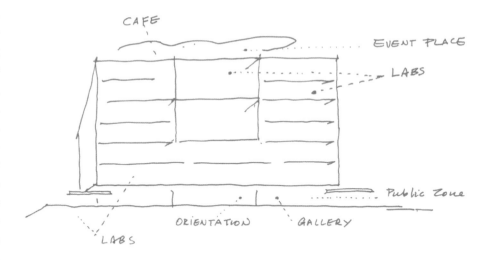

3 Sketch and models exploring functional and spatial organization.

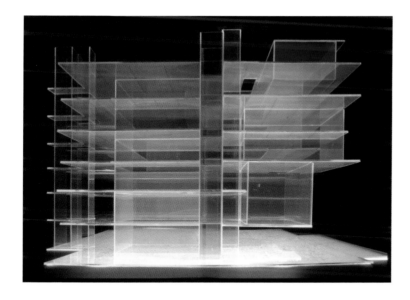

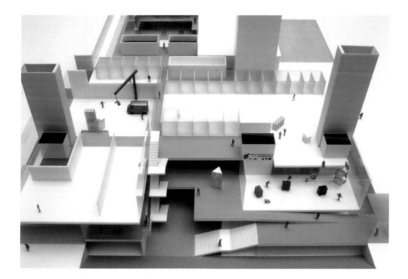

In the initial stages of a design I think in terms of "spatial entities" rather than thinking in terms of clear forms. . . . A spatial entity may suggest an overall image, but the edge conditions and the way the interior should be developed may still be undecided. It is the first task of design to determine the extent and character of the enclosed space.

–FUMIHIKO MAKI

the first occupants, and frequently demanded by managers as a justification for building and as a way of checking the architect's work—do not provide a rational basis for planning a research building that will operate for many decades in a highly dynamic environment.

Little more than a decade after its construction, the Wiesner Building was already obsolete and overcrowded, and the Media Laboratory needed a new building to accommodate its current activities adequately and provide for future expansion. But given its short history, and its unashamed positioning of itself against the general grain of MIT—for which many faculty members, administrators, and Corporation members still regarded it with suspicion—there was little chance that another building for the Media Laboratory would soon rise to the top of the Institute's construction priority list. So the director and his dean agreed to a much tougher deal with MIT's management than those that applied to the other major projects of the campus rebuilding effort; if they could raise the entire cost of the project from external sources, then they would get the go-ahead to build. The site was to be at the corner of Ames and Amherst streets, with the new building adjacent and connected to the Wiesner Building.

Fundraising got seriously under way as the technology boom of the late nineties gathered momentum, and the effort was soon rewarded with a gift of $25 million from Isao Okawa, founder of the Sega video game company. This provided sufficient confidence in the project to begin design work, and MIT awarded the commission to the distinguished Tokyo architect Fumihiko Maki. Maki was known for his ability to deal brilliantly with complex issues of site and program, for the restrained, minimalist elegance of his spaces, for the subtlety of his use of light, and for the refinement of his detailing. He had built widely in Japan and East Asia but had done little in the United States; this project would introduce his unique sensibility and extraordinary standards of

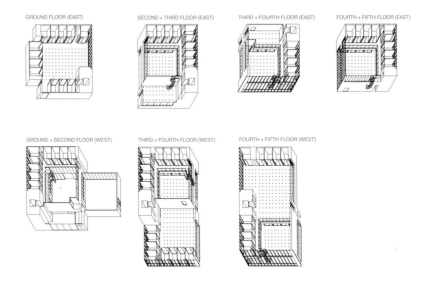

4 Axonometric projections of interlocking laboratory spaces, with offices clustered around shared, double-height working areas.

construction craftsmanship—deeply rooted in Japanese tradition and its complex intersections with industrial modernity—to a new context. It would add another strand of cultural connection to the campus of an institution that, as it had become increasingly global in its reach, had woven into its fabric John Ripley Freeman's American industrial pragmatism, Bosworth's allusions to Rome and to neoclassical French monumentality, Alvar Aalto's and Eero Saarinen's Finnish-tinged European modernism, I. M. Pei's suave internationalism, and Charles Correa's subtle evocation of the powerful stone planes of Mogul India.

In its massing, Maki's project defines the corner of Ames and Amherst, and it extends the block of the Wiesner building to form a bar parallel to those of Pei's Dreyfus Chemistry Building and the two

5 Perspective rendering of a laboratory space.

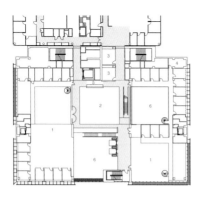

1 RESEARCH LABORATORY
2 UPPER ATRIUM
3 SMALL CONFERENCE
4 SERVER ROOM
5 KITCHENETTE
6 OPEN TO BELOW

THIRD FLOOR PLAN

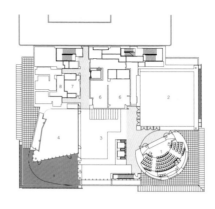

1 LECTURE HALL
2 EVENT SPACE
3 ANTEROOM "WINTER GARDEN"
4 LARGE CONFERENCE
5 ROOF TERRACE
6 KITCHEN
7 CLOAK
8 STORAGE

SIXTH FLOOR PLAN

1 RESEARCH LABORATORY
2 ADMINISTRATION/CASR
3 MEDIUM CONFERENCE
4 KITCHENETTE
5 STORAGE
6 SERVER ROOM
7 OPEN TO BELOW

SECOND FLOOR PLAN

1 RESEARCH LABORATORY
2 CAFE
3 MEDIUM CONFERENCE
4 EXHIBITION LOUNGE
5 STORAGE
6 SERVER ROOM
7 OPEN TO BELOW

FIFTH FLOOR PLAN

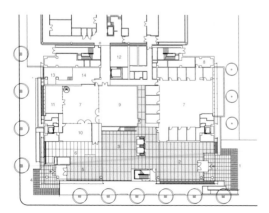

1 EAST ENTRY
2 EAST LOBBY EXHIBITION
3 LOWER ATRIUM
4 WEST ENTRY
5 WEST ENTRANCE HALL
6 EXHIBITION GALLERY
7 RESEARCH LABORATORY
8 SERVER ROOM
9 MACHINE SHOP
10 PRECISION FABRICATION
11 COMPOSITES
12 STORAGE
13 LOADING DOCK
14 RECEIVING AREA

GROUND FLOOR PLAN

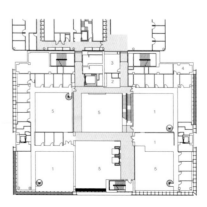

1 RESEARCH LABORATORY
2 KITCHENETTE
3 SMALL CONFERENCE
4 SERVER ROOM
5 OPEN TO BELOW

FOURTH FLOOR PLAN

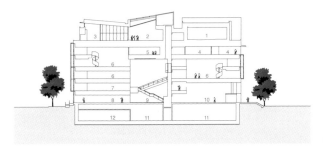

1 LECTURE HALL
2 ANTEROOM "WINTER GARDEN"
3 LARGE CONFERENCE
4 MEDIUM CONFERENCE
5 CAFE
6 RESEARCH LABORATORY
7 ADMINISTRATION / CASR
8 EXHIBITION GALLERY
9 LOWER ATRIUM
10 EAST LOBBY EXHIBITION
11 MECHANICAL SPACE
12 ELECTRICAL ROOM

EAST-WEST SECTION AT LOWER ATRIUM

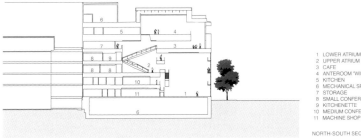

1 LOWER ATRIUM
2 UPPER ATRIUM
3 CAFE
4 ANTEROOM "WINTER GARDEN"
5 KITCHEN
6 MECHANICAL SPACE
7 STORAGE
8 SMALL CONFERENCE
9 KITCHENETTE
10 MEDIUM CONFERENCE
11 MACHINE SHOP

NORTH-SOUTH SECTION AT ATRIUM

6 Plans and sections.

dormitories facing it across Amherst Street. It also completes the framing of the quadrangle that had been begun with the Wiesner and Health Services Buildings. This sets up a powerful urban rhythm of bar buildings and quadrangles extending from Bosworth's Killian Court through Eastman Court and McDermott Court to Carleton Street—although the spaces to the east of that point remain ill defined and underdeveloped, and await shaping by future projects. It succeeds, while respecting its architectural integrity, in integrating Pei's singular pavilion back into the spatial patterns of the campus.

The front to Amherst Street is a witty and paradoxical play on Bosworth's Main Complex dome. There is a central axis, with massing disposed equally about it—but the volumes are displaced vertically, so that bilateral symmetry is broken and a rotational effect emerges instead. The crowning element is not a regular dome but a complex penthouse creating different silhouettes from different directions. The columns along the front create an elegant portico, but they are modernist rather than classical, and entry is from the sides instead of on the axis.

The skin of the building is a highly transparent, impeccably detailed curtain wall with external aluminum screens to control sun penetration, provide softly filtered daylight to the interior, create a scrimlike effect when viewed from the exterior at night, and establish a rhythm of larger-scale facade elements. It provides operable windows and spectacular views across the Charles River to the Boston skyline. In its delicacy and transparency, it becomes the light, bright yang to the solidity, opacity, and internal darkness of Pei's yin. The two halves of the resulting block-long mass are united by a tension of opposites rather than the classical device of repetition and symmetry.

The interior is complex, and you have to study the sections carefully to see exactly what is going on. Spaces have transparent edges, and they interlock vertically in surprising ways, providing not only

7 Views of atrium interiors.

horizontal vistas through layers of construction to the exterior, but also inclined ones—Maki's slyly twisted homage to the classical *enfilade* and the infinite corridor. A central atrium opens up to the view and sunlight to the south and provides glimpses into laboratories from its flying stairways and transparent elevators. Inverting conventional wisdom, the main attractors of public activity and population—auditoriums, meeting and event spaces, and a café—are located at the penthouse level, where they have the best views and also act to draw visitors up through the vertically stacked, transparent laboratory spaces so that the ongoing work is made visible.

Learning the lesson of the Wiesner Building, the laboratory and faculty office spaces do not respond to a specific program. There is simply as much laboratory space as the tight and valuable site can sustain under the city of Cambridge's planning regulations. It is modular and flexible, but varied in its spatial character and qualities of light and view. It carefully avoids dependence on technologies and assumptions that may become obsolete, but attempts to respond sensitively to basic human needs and desires that never change. And, with a couple of necessary exceptions, no names indicate specific uses of laboratory spaces on the drawings. Following the principle that code hackers know as late binding, uses will be assigned to spaces at the last possible moment before move-in and may be reassigned frequently after that.

As I wrote these words in 2006, the story of this project was coming to a cliffhanger of an ending driven by a backroom subplot that was not about intellectual ideals, architectural aspirations, or strategies of city building, but simply about access to capital. By June 2002, the promised external fundraising for the $125 million building had essentially been completed, the construction documents were done, the contractor had provided a guaranteed maximum price, the site had been cleared, and the building was scheduled to go into the ground.

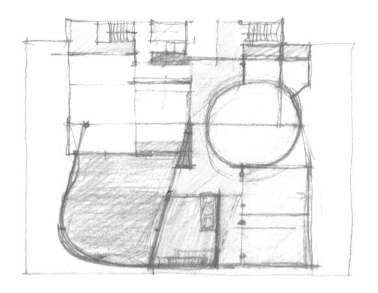

8 Plan sketch and perspective renderings of penthouse social and event spaces.

Then the economic bubble of the nineties burst, and two of the major donors were forced to rescind their promises of gifts, suddenly leaving a $50 million shortfall. It slowly emerged that this was part of a sad and complex story—one that was all too characteristic of the post-boom years. As their business empire had unraveled, these donors had defaulted on numerous philanthropic promises. Eventually, the story became even worse; they were arrested for fraud.[40]

Furthermore, construction costs in the Boston area were not declining, as one might expect, as the national economy generally headed down. The Big Dig project in downtown Boston—an enormous effort to put major roads underground and reconnect the city to its waterfront—was consuming local construction capacity and keeping prices high. Demand generated by China's urban construction boom was driving up global steel prices. And energy costs, which affect construction costs in multiple ways, continued to rise. MIT was caught in a squeeze.

The Media Laboratory's bold gamble on its fundraising ability in a rising economy had come within a hair's breadth of succeeding, only to fail dramatically at the very last moment. The construction schedule was suspended, Maki responded appropriately by reducing the program and stripping about $30 million out of the project while maintaining—perhaps even enhancing—its essential architectural qualities, and the fundraisers got back to work on the remaining $20 million in a much more difficult economic climate. The project leaders argued that MIT should take some debt to provide bridging funds and allow the project to go ahead while fundraising proceeded, but the Corporation—mindful that it was facing a massive decline in the value of MIT's endowment as a result of the same economic downturn—refused. Money had talked to get the project moving, and now money spoke to stop it. Some saw this as prudent fiscal restraint; others saw it as a disastrous failure of institutional nerve at a moment of adversity.

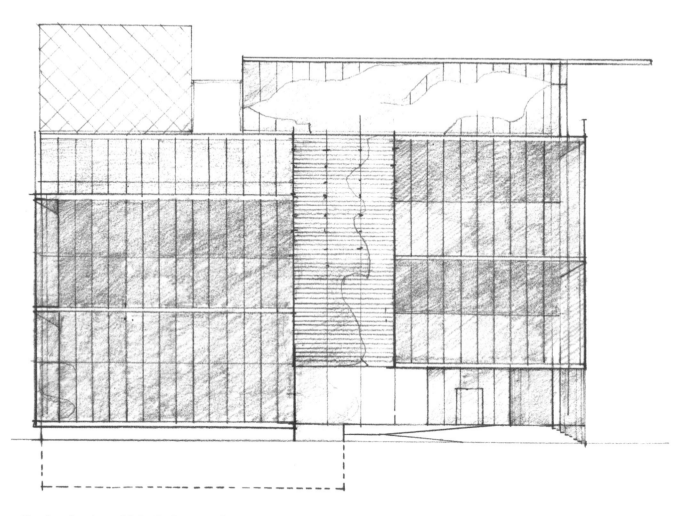

9 Sketch and study model detail of exterior aluminum screen.

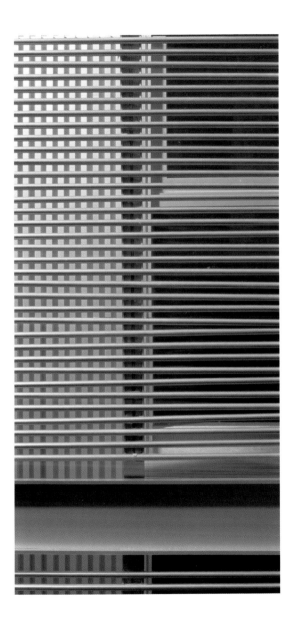

Weeds grew on the empty and deserted construction site. The funding gap grew by another $20 million as construction costs continued to rise. The originators of the project moved on to new jobs, the design and construction team dispersed, the lead donor died, and the contractor went out of business. It seemed increasingly likely that Maki's exquisite project would become, like Tatlin's tower in Saint Petersburg or Le Corbusier's League of Nations, a poignantly unbuilt monument to the possibilities of a vanished time.

Then, in July 2006, a lurking deus ex machina made its move. After secretive negotiations, an anonymous donor provided the major gift needed to start construction. The architects began to update the project documentation, and MIT scheduled a construction start for 2007. The tale of this project had seemed headed for a *House of Atreus* ending; suddenly, with a last-minute plot twist that would embarrass a Hollywood rewrite team, it went *Sound of Music*. This time-shifted finale marked the end of an architectural era at MIT. The cycle of questioning, exploration, and innovation that had begun with Zesiger, and continued through Simmons Hall, the Stata Center, and BCSC, had come to its conclusion; henceforth, campus building would be driven by different conditions, personalities, and priorities.

When one designs space from the inside, one must eventually confront the issue of the membrane at the boundary between interior space and the external environment. Only when one has fully faced up to that question, does the work of architecture begin. In order to construct a desired space as architectural reality, one must begin to think "how." This leads to a quest to find the most appropriate and expressive ways of designing structural and fenestration systems. One must search for the most appropriate materials and then develop details that will link these materials to form a coherent architectural entity.
—FUMIHIKO MAKI

It isn't what you might expect of an institution dedicated to scientific problem solving; the MIT campus has not resulted from orderly application of technological rationality driven by clear, shared goals. Its creation has been a much more complex, contentious, episodic process of imaginatively projecting possibilities, debating priorities, engaging cultural crosscurrents, seizing on emerging economic and political opportunities, and responding to the unexpected. Sometimes this has worked well, sometimes not—but, in general, MIT today is much the better for it.

When John Ripley Freeman conceived of a New Tech on the banks of the Charles, his idea was simply to establish a comprehensive master plan and then implement it. This seemed clear and logical, but things did not work out as he hoped; his scheme was aborted before a shovel hit the ground. Many of the Freeman plan's most powerful ideas, however, carried over into Bosworth's later and more successful scheme. Bosworth produced numerous versions of his vision, and it was gradually transformed—through numerous additions, deletions, and modifications—over the decades of its staged implementation. At the end of his long and honor-filled life, in 1961, Bosworth was still pressing, unsuccessfully, to add the statue of Minerva—the "necktie" of his composition. In the postwar years, the newer laboratory buildings that were appended to Bosworth's complex preserved the abstract principles of the quadrangle, the infinite corridor system, and the uniform planning module, but dispensed with the symmetry, the limestone, and the classical skin. Master plans proved not to be stable frameworks for future design and construction, but provisional codifications of ideas that might or might not survive changing conditions and critical scrutiny at future moments. Generally, ideas carried forward selectively, with some dropping away over time and new ones appearing.

A less brittle device than a master plan is a set of policies, standards, and guidelines—much like the provisions of municipal building and planning codes—that ensure some consistency in design and construction. But such abstractions lack the power to fire the imagination. Without the force of law and effective enforcement mechanisms behind them, they are difficult to keep in place as successive generations of leadership take over, and as memories of their original rationales fade. Often, they are more about naive notions of brand maintenance than architecture, and they reduce to the triviality of mandating consistent coatings of historically sanctioned materials and motifs on buildings that are, internally, quite different. They have always conflicted with the modernist strategy of clearly expressing differentiated internal functions on the exterior, and they have forced architects to work within formal idioms that might once have seemed fresh, but have since become stale and clichéd—much like forcing James Joyce to write in the cadences of Edward Bulwer-Lytton. For all of these reasons, formalized architectural and planning guidelines have had little traction in the century-long evolution of the MIT campus— and a good thing, too; otherwise the Institute might still, like an aging architectural cross-dresser, be squeezing itself into increasingly weary pastiches of Bosworth.

1 An urban design charette conducted in March 1999 to develop alternative scenarios for the future of the MIT campus. Participants included Charles Correa, Harry Ellenzweig, Frank Gehry, Jim Glymph, Steven Holl, Tunney Lee, Fumihiko Maki, William Mitchell, Laurie Olin, and Robert Simha.

A third alternative is to attempt emulation of the thoughtful and resourceful sailor—to read as insightfully as possible the gathering, changing, and largely uncontrollable forces that are shaping and reshaping emerging circumstances, to make quick and necessarily context-dependent determinations of how to harness these forces to good effect while managing the risks that they present, and all the while to steer determinedly in the direction of fundamental social and urbanistic goals. This is real-time planning, and it is the approach that has guided MIT's campus building at its best. It has enabled at least a few works of great architectural distinction, and it has produced a richly varied—sometimes wonderfully idiosyncratic—urban texture.

Real-time planning strategies explicitly oppose themselves to the ideology of comprehensive rational planning—as rather chillingly exemplified by John Ripley Freeman's totalizing Taylorism. They have more in common with incrementalism—the science of muddling through—in Charles Lindblom's famous phrase.[41] But they place greater emphasis than classic incrementalism on responding to the uniqueness of the cultural moment and its opportunities, the necessity of continually challenging and destabilizing frozen assumptions, and the sheer joy of imaginative invention. They emphasize resourceful bricolage with the spaces, material opportunities, and political and cultural potentials that happen to present themselves.

Successful real-time planning cannot be done by rote. It depends on an institution's willingness to treat each architectural project, as it emerges, as an opportunity both for critical reflection on the past and for inventive exploration of options for the future. It requires engagement of the full range and complexity of architectural and urbanistic goals, and it is fundamentally incompatible with reductionist framing of projects solely in terms of capital budgets, schedules, and rigid, bureaucratically determined space programs: real estate procurement,

project scheduling, and facility management do not add up to urbanism. It rests on a wide-ranging, well-informed, adventurous architect selection process that seeks challenging intellectual partners rather than compliant technicians or trophy prima donnas, draws on the best talent available internationally, and carefully matches the skills and sensibilities of designers to the conditions and requirements of particular projects. It recognizes that, in the tired but true Churchillian phrase, we make our buildings and then our buildings make us.

It requires setting clear goals and appropriate incentives for internal facilities groups and project managers. These perform useful management functions, but in doing so they interpose themselves between the client leaders and their architects. Furthermore, they are understandably averse to anything that creates risk of failure to meet budget and schedule targets, but this has a downside; great architecture is impossible without taking some considered risks, and without trying to realize the maximum architectural and urban benefit out of the available land and financial resources. So, if campus leaders want adventurous innovation—not just smoothly managed mediocrity—they cannot afford to delegate too much initiative and crucial decision making to this level. They must make their high expectations clear; they must recruit managers with the skill, commitment, and courage to follow through on them; and they must take direct, informed responsibility for the tough, high-level decisions that set overall project directions.

The ultimate success of real-time planning also depends on a clear and consistently applied understanding of where value truly lies. There is value in designing attentively, imaginatively, and well, but this takes more time and effort than pursuing the most obvious solutions, so it will cost a little more. There is value in building well, which will generally increase the initial cost of a project but greatly decrease the lifetime cost—which makes sense for an institution that is not building speculatively, but will be a long-term owner. There is value in providing windows that open to admit fresh air, even though the mechanical consultants will tell you that it's difficult and expensive. And there is value in being properly skeptical of value engineers. At their best they are shrewd professionals who can find the most efficient ways to accomplish what's needed in a project, and show how to allocate available resources to greatest advantage, but all too often they are simply cost-cutters who know the price of everything and the value of nothing.

It is crucial, in general, to understand the logic of investment at the margin. Aiming for high design and construction quality generally adds only a small percentage to the initial cost of a project, but pays off disproportionately in terms of benefits realized over the long lifetime of a building. Conversely, penny-pinching at the margin can disproportionately diminish a project's long-term payoff—producing a blight that lasts for decades, like a bad smell that refuses to go away.

Within the framework of real-time planning, decisions to build must be carefully considered relative to available resources, other demands on these resources, and the current economic climate. Once they are made, however, it's best to get on with it. If a project is long delayed, the ultimate costs will almost certainly rise substantially with no corresponding architectural or urban benefit—or, if the initial cost targets are maintained, there will be a reduction in scale and quality of the building that eventually results. If a project is canceled at an advanced stage, there will be major loss of sunk costs, and donors who have made gifts in the expectation that the project will go ahead will begin to ask for their money back.

The great advantage of a well-executed real-time planning strategy, in the end, is its flexibility. It avoids the mechanistic application of received general principles and provides opportunities to respond sensitively and imaginatively to emerging needs, varied architectural and urban contexts, and situationally expressed opportunities. The greatest potential disadvantage is that, without strong leadership and passionate commitment to the highest architectural and urban ideals, it can lose its way—degenerating, as MIT campus building too often has, into sequences of narrowly framed, opportunistic projects that don't contribute to the formation of a larger social and architectural whole. It is particularly easy to neglect the commons—the social spaces, communal places, and infrastructural elements that are important to the community and its culture, but don't fit within the scopes of projects that serve more sectional constituencies. Indeed, it is in the narrow interests of fundraising, budget-managing deans and laboratory directors to exclude these sorts of things from their projects whenever possible.

Institutional structures that preserve a critical sense of campus history, urban context, and long-range goals can provide effective safeguards against these inherent dangers. These can ensure continuity of architecturally sophisticated thinking, expertise, and advocacy focused on overall campus design—providing, where necessary, the voice of cultural and urban conscience in the tough debates that accompany a university's decision making on major capital projects. It helps, as well, to establish budgetary processes that give sufficient weight to long-term value and sustainability and not just short-term targets and constraints. And continual injection of fresh new ideas is crucial; there is no substitute for frequent, disruptive, uncomfortable design interventions—particularly from periodic urban design exercises that put all assumptions on the table for reconsideration and freely construct compelling scenarios for the future.

Most of all, real-time planning is the art of the not obviously possible. Leaders must recognize that projects are framed by unique combinations of personalities, motives, and economic and political opportunities and constraints, that this framing will produce contradictions and conflicts, and that finding a way forward to innovative architecture—not just a project that represents the easiest consensus—requires energetic, clear-sighted, resourceful negotiation. The initial occupants will be an essential source of insight about user needs, and will see the project as their future home; but they will, in fact, inhabit the completed building for only a tiny fraction of its long life in a changing environment, so their demands cannot be accepted uncritically. Donors must be sought out and convinced, but they will sometimes turn out to have goals that aren't aligned with those of other stakeholders, and may, furthermore, want to leverage the effects of their gifts in institutionally uncomfortable ways. Determined and articulate professors who don't directly benefit from projects will promote alternative uses of the funding, creating pressure to cost-cut in irrational ways just to keep them quiet. Managers responsible for execution on tight budgets and schedules will sometimes see creative architects as potential trouble. Neighbors will vigorously represent their own interests, often in highly adversarial fashion, by political and legal means—which creates a temptation not to rock the boat in any way. When it is all done, everyone doesn't end up with everything he or she wanted, so the project leaders must be prepared to absorb some complaints from the disappointed. Out of all this, they must create constructive common ground.

In sum, real-time planning recognizes that opportunities to build on a campus do not emerge in an orderly and predictable way, but are the joint product of the highly uncertain ebbs and flows of capital, the largely unpredictable development of new research priorities, and the changing and not always rational political winds of large and complex organizations. Like the science on which MIT is grounded, real-time planning refuses the uncritical extrapolation of the past, but critiques

and tests its patrimony at every opportunity; this produces an intellectual trajectory that is sometimes incremental and even routine but on occasion admits dramatic reconsideration, reframing, and redirection. It respects tradition, but prizes invention even more. It disdains cosmetic unity and seeks, instead, a vivid discourse across the generations that inherit stewardship of the patch of land and its growing accumulation of architectural interventions.

Inevitably, real-time planning has its victories, its defeats, and its indecisive struggles. It generally doesn't come out quite the way the principal protagonists in the process expect, but that usually isn't such a bad thing. It is realistic about uncertainty, and it recognizes democracy's precarious balance of cooperation and conflict. In spirit, it leans more to a diverse, immigrant nation's Walt Whitman—with his generous delight in multiplicity, contradiction, and the difficult and provisional whole—than to the Enlightenment consistency and certainty of Thomas Jefferson.

AFTERWORD: TRANSFORMING THE MIT CAMPUS—
A PERSONAL JOURNEY

Charles M. Vest
President Emeritus

Great universities evolve intellectually, socially, and physically roughly 50 percent by planning and 50 percent by serendipity. An academic institution is not like an orchestra with a president as conductor. MIT is more like a jam session among a lot of talented musicians who listen to each other and get into the flow. The president, provost, deans, and other administrators strive to hire the right "musicians," draw the themes from the evolving music, and keep the beat going. The art lies in recognizing newly emerging intellectual areas as strategic opportunities and moments, and forging the institutional momentum and resources to bring vision to reality. It was in this context that MIT's campus was imagined and then transformed as it passed from the twentieth century to the twenty-first.

The iconic view of MIT is its domed and pillared Maclaurin Building facing south toward the Charles River. I fell in love with—and in awe of—this sight on my morning jogs along the banks of the Charles as I passed Killian Court and the grand buildings designed in the early twentieth century by William Welles Bosworth. Cutting behind the west campus dormitories, passing by Alvar Aalto's Baker House, and returning to the president's house would leave me inspired and prepared for the day ahead. Each morning the quality of light was different, but there was always a sense of grandeur, stateliness, and importance.

The north side of the campus, facing into the city of Cambridge, was another matter. My first drive down Vassar Street in 1990 was a shock. Here were dark spaces, run-down buildings, fifty-year-old asbestos shingles, and chain link fences. Having arrived at MIT with a great reverence for it, I could not connect what I saw on Vassar Street with what I knew to be the excellence and innovation of the institution. At some level neither this scene nor the stateliness of the Bosworth buildings seemed to reflect the extraordinary and forward-looking reality, excitement, and electricity of what went on inside.

It was clear that the campus needed to reflect that innovation and excellence far better than it did at the time. What was not so clear was whether we would have the resources to make any significant improvements during my tenure. As it turned out, when I left office after fourteen years as president, we had constructed six major buildings comprising about 25 percent of the square footage on the MIT campus. We also had thoroughly renovated several buildings and lovingly restored Baker House.

The fact is that since MIT moved from Boston to Cambridge in 1916, the opportunity for development and renewal of the campus has come in waves every twenty or thirty years. There are good reasons for this. First and foremost, this cycle is driven by the economy. When the economy gets better, one can accomplish things. When the economy gets worse, one has to pull back. Juxtaposed with this are the intellectual trends—what faculty are doing and aspiring to—especially in a university focused largely on science and technology. Evolving views of campus life and modalities of teaching and learning also create opportunities for rethinking the physical spaces of a campus.

The pivotal moment came in 1997–1998 when it became obvious that we had an opportunity and obligation to create things of historical import in the development of MIT, both intellectually and physically. There was not a singularly well-formed vision; however, as Louis Pasteur famously observed, "Chance favors the well-prepared mind." Many MIT minds were well prepared to recognize and act on a unique period of opportunity.

What were some of the inputs? As the new millennium approached, books with titles like *The End of Science* appeared, but in reality we had entered the most exciting period for science and technology in human history. On the MIT campus alone, faculty were pursuing extraordinary new opportunities to meld life sciences with physical and information sciences and to deepen understanding of the human brain and the nature of intelligence. Neuroscience, molecular genetics, systems biology, and nanoscale science and technology were rapidly evolving new areas that were bringing faculty and students together across disciplinary boundaries. Energy, environment, and sustainable development demanded new approaches to large, complex systems and to social, economic, and engineering solutions. It was a yeasty time, rich with promise and responsibility.

In 1998, the MIT Task Force on Student Life and Learning issued an important report. This faculty group had been chartered two years earlier to consider what kind of education and experience we owed our remarkable students in the years ahead. Somewhat unexpectedly, the report did not focus in detail on the intellectual content of the curriculum. After deliberating, conducting surveys, and interviewing many students, faculty, and alumni, the task force concluded that MIT should stop thinking of itself as resting on the two pillars of teaching and research. Rather, they believed that MIT's foundation should be a triad: *academics*, *research*, and *community*. We needed to become a better-integrated academic community and attenuate the severe separation that had evolved between the environments in which students lived and the environments in which they learned.

This report did not gather dust on a shelf. It shaped our budget and influenced a restructuring of our administration. It was reflected in campus planning and in the projected architectural nature of our buildings and spaces.

Undergirding all of this was a dramatic and relatively rapid restructuring of our financial foundation. It was clear that we needed to reduce our dependence on federally sponsored research funds and develop a more balanced set of resources, drawing much more on the private sector in the form of both industry support and private philanthropy. We began building that foundation, even as we worked to reinvigorate our partnership with the government. This included assembling a great team of people in the administration that would be oriented to plan and deliver the changes necessary to respond to the challenges and opportunities before us.

In 1998, I wrote and distributed an essay titled *The Path to Our Future*. This essay was not just a personal view; it reflected what I had heard and learned from many different quarters in the institution. It was about core function. It was about what it takes to attract and empower great faculty—and great students—to do what they think is important. It was about what would be required in the new century to advance our role as an institution that looks outward, meets bold challenges, and influences the world in positive and important ways. It also recognized a major role for transformation of our campus to better shape the future—to make MIT a brighter place without diminishing the intensity and rigor that define us.

In transforming a campus, the right balance must be struck between continuity and change. We thus built on the dedicated work of people like Bob Simha, our campus planner for many years, and Bill Dickson, who was our senior vice president. But Bill Mitchell played a singular role as architectural advisor to the president. His wisdom and his bal-

ance—not pushing things, but showing opportunity and alternatives—meant a lot to me personally and benefited our campus enormously.

The selection of Frank Gehry to design a new home for computer science, the Ray and Maria Stata Center, was pivotal. With the help of Bill Mitchell and Vicky Sirianni, MIT's chief facilities officer, we established a formal selection process. Some twenty architects were invited to propose designs for what we knew was a critically important project. Every one of them expressed interest. A committee of faculty and administrators first narrowed the list down to six finalists—two world-class architects, two fine but familiar architects, and two young up-and-comers—and then ultimately to two. I met with this committee when it was ready with its report and asked each person to tell me which of the two finalists they thought we should select and why. Lo and behold, there was a 50/50 split between two architects.

The president of a university may claim to sit in an office and make a lot of major decisions, but the fact is one doesn't really do that very often. Teamwork and consensus building are more the norm. But here we had a moment when the decision rested solely with me. I sat down at my office coffee table with that wonderful and wise colleague Bill Dickson, who had led MIT construction almost since he had graduated as a student. I knew in my heart that I wanted to go with Frank Gehry, because we had to do something big, bold, exciting, and different to lead into the new century. I resolved that if I could convince Bill that this was the thing to do, I would know that it was the right decision. We chatted a while, and I told Bill my thinking. He was silent for a minute and then said, "Well, let me tell you something. When our Chapel was designed by Eero Saarinen, it was considered so radical that the sponsoring foundation pulled its funding from it. Well, look at how proud we are of it today." I said, "Sounds like we know who we need." He said, "Right, let's get . . ." and I said, "You make the call."

Of course Frank Gehry would produce a remarkable facility for us, but was there a risk that he would not listen to the faculty clients in the right way? We did not need a signature architect for the sake of having a signature architect. The building had to reflect what we are and what we do, and above all it had to be a wonderful yet practical place for our faculty, students, and staff to learn and work. It had to support the intellectual changes and new styles of research of the coming decades.

After Bill's initial call, I phoned Frank Gehry. We talked for twenty-five minutes, but about twenty of those minutes were consumed by him telling me stories about the brilliant and iconoclastic physicist Richard Feynman. That signaled to me that he really understood what places like MIT are about. He clearly understood the significance of replacing Building 20, which had housed so many historic and mythic MIT people and activities. I hung up feeling great confidence that we would get what we wanted and needed.

It was years ago when I was a kid. I used to go to a friend's New Year's party, and a bunch of people from Cal Tech used to go there, and there was a guy who was dancing wildly and all of us were pretty heavily drinking . . . and at six in the morning I was sitting on the floor next to him watching the sunrise. I realized he wasn't drunk at all. He was a real poet and he was very excited about the aesthetics of the sunrise and the physics of it.

–FRANK GEHRY

Peter Reich, who headed the psychiatric service in the MIT medical department, said to me one day, "You know MIT is the best place in the world to be a psychiatrist. In most venues, if you're a shrink, people come to your office, turn up the collar of their overcoat, look at their shoes, and hem and haw. It takes two or three visits before they get around to saying what is bothering them. But at MIT, people just stride into my office, look in my eyes and think, 'I'll bet he's as good at being a psychiatrist as I am at being a computer scientist.' So they just tell me what the trouble is and we go to work."

With that in mind I built a theory of "faith-based campus development"; that is, get the right people for the right reason and let them do their jobs. This is about function, not about monuments. It's about enabling, inspiring, respecting, and reflecting what we do, but also about raising our sights. I deeply believe that the new campus environment created by Kevin Roche's Zesiger Center, Steven Holl's Simmons Hall, Frank Gehry's Stata Center, Charles Correa's Brain and Cognitive Sciences Complex, and Fumihiko Maki's Media Laboratory will raise the sights of generations of students and faculty as well as reflect and enable what they do. Above all, this new environment displays boldness and confidence in MIT's future.

To be honest, this was not an easy task. It was necessary to build a new team to support our chief facilities officer. There were natural complexities of matching the passion and visions of donors to academic needs and necessary financial time frames. Vigorous debates had to be enjoined with our trustees to balance investment in facilities against financial investment for endowment growth. Architects and construction firms had to have their feet held to the fire to contain costs even as we had to convince colleagues that extra investments were necessary to bring new brightness, inspiration, and social spaces. Some members of our extended campus community, having seen only renderings, concluded that many of the buildings were ugly and counter to MIT tradition. A newspaper columnist who refused to admit that he had confused the number of square feet with the price of one building spread exaggerated statements about cost. An alumnus and property owner whose business abutted Steven Holl's dormitory used legal maneuvers that caused us to miss a critical construction deadline by a year. Above all, we constantly had to weigh the importance of the physical campus against the daunting challenges of student financial aid, rising health care and housing costs, renovation of existing facilities, and seeding new educational and research programs.

Once the campus transformation started in earnest, I began to think of myself as a snapping turtle. I had to grab people and events by the ankle and not let go until the job was done. So many constituencies came into play, among them faculty, students, trustees, alumni, donors, and the federal government. And we had to deal with enormous external forces, especially the vagaries of the economy. When we started, we were empowered to be bold because the economy had accelerated upward. But the laws of economics had not been repealed by the dot-com phenomenon, so just as we got deeply into the construction, the economy turned down. I learned a lot about perseverance.

One day, when our building program was well under way, MIT's Academic Council and a few other friends toured all the construction and renovation projects. As I was leaving at the end of the tour, one of my colleagues said to me, "It must really make you happy to see all this going on." I looked at him and said, "The truth is, it has been so hard and so painful to keep going that I don't feel very happy right now." But today the transformed campus has begun to accomplish its purposes, and time and success have replaced angst with a sense of accomplishment. The new spaces are filled with people, machines, ideas, and the excitement of exploring the new and unknown. It is a place of brightness, community, and color as well as intensity, discovery, and rigor.

Building things is an act of will. The original creation of MIT was an act of will. This was landfill. They moved out of the area of Copley Square in Boston to come here because they believed something. They knew they couldn't build it all immediately, but they built it over time. Over time, cities change. Universities change. You're going to build things no matter what, so you need a kind of road map to get somewhere. You can't be sure where it will take you; by the time everything's done, it will probably look different from what you imagined. But you've got to start somewhere, and have the courage to aim high enough, so that by the time you scale back to what actually gets done, it's still something to be proud of. And then you just have to go for it.

–LAURIE OLIN

NOTES

INTRODUCTION

1. Many smaller projects—some of considerable architectural significance—also contributed to the transformation. These included major renovations to the School of Architecture and Planning, the MIT Museum, Alvar Aalto's Baker House, Eero Saarinen's Kresge Auditorium and Chapel, Lobby 7 of William Welles Bosworth's Main Complex, I. M. Pei's Dreyfus chemistry building, and a courtyard insert building in the Main Complex for the Department of Physics. In addition, there were two major planning studies: Laurie Olin produced a comprehensive landscape plan and campus design framework, and the team of Payette Associates and Robert Venturi generated a plan for the incremental rehabilitation of the Main Complex.

2. For a notably pessimistic view of the future of residential universities and their campuses, published just before MIT began its rebuilding, see Eli M. Noam, "Electronics and the Dim Future of the University," *Science* 270 (October 13, 1995): 247–249. For a more nuanced view, see Frank H. T. Rhodes, "The New University," chapter 13 of *The Creation of the Future: The Role of the American University* (Ithaca: Cornell University Press, 2001), pp. 229–244.

3. I came to MIT from Harvard in 1992, and served as dean of the School of Architecture and Planning until 2003.

4. Charles M. Vest served as president of MIT from 1990 until December 2004. For a profile see web.mit.edu/president/communications/profile.html.

1. THE AMERICAN CAMPUS

5. Le Corbusier, *When the Cathedrals Were White* (New York: McGraw-Hill, 1964), p. 135 (translated from the French edition of 1937).

6. The usage dates from the 1770s. Before this, the terms "yard" (as at Harvard) and "grounds" were favored. See Paul Venable Turner, *Campus: An American Planning Tradition* (Cambridge: MIT Press, 1984), p. 47.

7. For a comprehensive account, with numerous examples, see Turner, *Campus.*

8. The plan evolved over a number of years, and Benjamin Henry Latrobe made the key suggestion of adding a monumental domed structure. See Turner, *Campus*, pp. 76–87.

9. For a cogent overview of these dynamics in the 1990s and 2000s, see Charles M. Vest, *The American Research University from World War II to World Wide Web* (Berkeley: University of California Press, 2007), chapters 1 and 2.

2. WILLIAM WELLES BOSWORTH: TAYLORISM AND CLASSICISM

10. For the early history of MIT's Cambridge campus, I have relied mostly upon Mark Jarzombek's research, published in *Designing MIT: Bosworth's New Tech* (Boston: Northeastern University Press, 2004).

11. Frederick Winslow Taylor, *The Principles of Scientific Management* (New York: Dover, 1998) (originally New York: Harper & Brothers, 1911).

12. Reyner Banham explored the connection between Durand and modernism in *Theory and Design in the First Machine Age*, 2nd ed. (Cambridge: MIT Press, 1980).

3. POSTWAR PRAGMATISM

13. Building 20 inspired much affection among its inhabitants, and it played an important role in sixties campus counterculture. Stewart Brand wrote an ode to it in *How Buildings Learn* (New York: Viking Penguin, 1994).

14. These were published as the *MIT Radiation Laboratory Series* (New York: McGraw-Hill, 1947–1948).

15. Vannevar Bush, *Science: The Endless Frontier: A Report to the President on a Program for Postwar Scientific Research* (1945; reprinted, Washington, D.C.: National Science Foundation, 1990).

16. L. E. Grinter et al., "Report of the Committee on Evaluation of Engineering Education," *Engineering Education* 45 (September 1955): 25–60.

17. Much of the story is recounted, with extensive illustrations, in O. Robert Simha, *MIT Campus Planning 1960–2000* (Cambridge: MIT Press, 2001).

4. ALVAR AALTO AND EERO SAARINEN: MIDCENTURY MODERNISM

18. Joseph Hudnut, "On Form in Universities," *Architectural Forum*, December 1947, pp. 88–93. Richard Dober later developed the process view of campus planning, in great detail, in *Campus Planning* (New York: Reinhold, 1968).

19. This structural perversity was immediately pointed out, with distaste, by the great engineer Pier Luigi Nervi. He commented: "I could demonstrate that structural thought and common sense have been allied in all ages. Today structural ideas are invaded by extravagance, and they are deprived of all justification." See "Three Critics Discuss MIT's New Buildings," *Architectural Forum*, March 1956, p. 157.

20. Flo Conway and Jim Siegelman, *Dark Hero of the Information Age: In Search of Norbert Wiener, the Father of Cybernetics* (New York: Basic Books, 2004), p. 306.

21. Quoted in Thomas H. Creighton, "The Sixties: A P/A Symposium on the State of Architecture," *Progressive Architecture*, March 1961, p. 122. I am indebted to Eeva-Liisa Pelkonen for drawing my attention to the critical reception of Saarinen's MIT projects; see her *Eero Saarinen: Shaping the Future* (New Haven: Yale University Press, forthcoming).

22. The phrase is that of the contemporary architect and critic Robin Boyd in "Counter Revolution in Architecture," *Harper's Magazine*, September 1959, p. 44.

23. Quoted in Pelkonen, *Eero Saarinen,* from an unpublished manuscript in the Eero Saarinen Papers, Yale University.

24. Quoted in "Three Critics Discuss MIT's New Buildings," *Architectural Forum*, March 1956, p. 157.

5. KEVIN ROCHE: ZESIGER SPORTS AND FITNESS CENTER

25. *Report of the MIT Task Force on Student Life and Learning*, September 1998, http://web.mit.edu/committees/sll/tf.html.

26. The Zesigers, in whose honor the Center was named, were committed lifetime athletes and had long been strong supporters of athletics at MIT.

27. Every architect who looks at the space ends up trying to complete Saarinen's vision in this way. Harry Weese developed a proposal in the 1960s, for example, and Charles Correa did so in the 2000s.

6. STEVEN HOLL: SIMMONS HALL

28. Ancient, quasi-monastic universities had grounded community in shared religious faith. Their secular successors had frequently relied upon extensive humanities cores to establish common intellectual ground. These traditional mechanisms had never operated at MIT, and the problem of community had been exacerbated by the subdivision of science and engineering into increasingly narrow specializations and the fragmentation of living arrangements. On the general issue of creating and sustaining community on research university campuses, see Frank H. T. Rhodes, "Restoring Community," chapter 4 of *The Creation of the Future: The Role of the American University* (Ithaca: Cornell University Press, 2001), pp. 45–57.

29. Ibid.

30. Richard P. Simmons graduated from MIT in 1953 and pursued a successful career in metallurgy and metals manufacturing and processing. Simmons and his wife Dorothy made the gift jointly. In his gift letter to Vest, Simmons wrote: "For MIT to continue to provide the kind of educational experience necessary to retain its worldwide reputation as an outstanding university, it must be willing to allocate resources specifically focused on quality of life issues at MIT."

31. For further details of the design and its development, see Todd Gannon and Michael Denison, eds., *Steven Holl: Simmons Hall* (New York: Princeton Architectural Press, 2004).

32. These are from James Howard Kunstler, *Eyesore of the Month*, February 2004, www.kunstler.com/eyesore_200402.html, last accessed July 13, 2006.

33. Robert Campbell, "Like No Building You've Ever Seen Before," *Boston Globe*, February 20, 2005.

7. FRANK GEHRY: STATA CENTER

34. For further details see Nancy E. Joyce, *Building Stata: The Design and Construction of Frank O. Gehry's Stata Center at MIT* (Cambridge: MIT Press, 2004), and William J. Mitchell, "Roll Over Euclid: How Frank Gehry Designs and Builds," in *Frank Gehry, Architect*, ed. J. Fiona Ragheb (New York: Harry N. Abrams, 2003), pp. 352–364.

35. Even if there had been cars, early universities would not have needed much parking space, since they functioned as self-contained residential communities. But, as universities evolved into large organizations drawing students and employees from throughout extensive, automobile-serviced metropolitan areas, the demand for on-campus parking grew rapidly. Long before suburban shopping centers, campuses became drive-to destinations. This became an increasingly significant campus planning issue as parking lots and structures grew into problematic features of campus landscapes, and as nearby residents worried about traffic. Surface parking does not go well with quadrangles, large parking structures disrupt pedestrian movement and street life, and less conspicuous peripheral parking lots are unpopular with those who have to walk to and from them. The difficulty has been particularly acute at MIT, where the high water table of the filled wetland on which the campus is built makes the obvious alternative, underground parking, extremely expensive to construct.

36. According to published figures, for example, the University of Washington's Paul G. Allen Center for Computer Science and Engineering—a 2003 building with similar functions but a much more traditional, brick-clad form—cost about 30 percent more per square foot than Stata.

8. CHARLES CORREA: BRAIN AND COGNITIVE SCIENCES COMPLEX

37. In the end, it turned out that the detailed layout of the laboratory floors was determined as much by the politics of space allocation and turf definition as by this clear and attractive architectural principle. Laboratories are subdivided into small, enclosed areas rather than left as large, flexible spaces.

And many researchers demanded meeting spaces internal to their areas, diminishing the principle of meeting and interaction at the boundaries.

38. Robert Campbell, "Studying the Brain in a Building of Understated Beauty," *Boston Globe*, December 18, 2005.

9. FUMIHIKO MAKI: MEDIA LABORATORY

39. The research focus of the Media Laboratory, at its height, was vividly delineated by Nicholas Negroponte in *Being Digital* (New York: Knopf, 1995). Stewart Brand enthusiastically evoked its ethos in *The Media Lab: Inventing the Future at MIT* (New York: Viking, 1987).

40. James B. Stewart, "The Opera Lover: The Fall of Alberto Vilar," *New Yorker*, February 13/20, 2006.

10. PLANNING A CAMPUS IN REAL TIME

41. Charles E. Lindblom, "The Science of 'Muddling Through'," *Public Administration Review* 19, no. 2 (1959): 79–88

SOURCES OF SIDEBAR QUOTES

page

2   Letter of May 6, 1810, in Andrew Adgate Lipscomb and Albert Ellery Bergh, eds., *The Writings of Thomas Jefferson* (Washington, D.C.: Thomas Jefferson Memorial Association, 1903), 2:386–388.

6   Frederick Winslow Taylor, *The Principles of Scientific Managment* (New York: Dover, 1998), p. 74 (originally New York: Harper and Brothers, 1911).

9   Notes attached to Freeman's perspective view.

18 Transcript of the 2004 Max Wasserman Forum "The University as a Patron of Cutting Edge Architecture," sponsored by the List Visual Arts Center, MIT, May 8, 2004.

33 Quoted in John Peter, *The Oral History of Modern Architecture* (New York: Harry N. Abrams, 1994), p. 194.

35 Peter, *The Oral History of Modern Architecture,* pp. 197–198.

36 Transcript from MIT campus planning charette, March 1999.

41 Kevin Roche, personal communication to William Mitchell, March 9, 2006.

42 Kevin Roche, notes on the Zesiger Center prepared in 2005.

45 Kevin Roche, notes on the Zesiger Center prepared in 2005.

48 From an interview published in Todd Gannon and Michael Denison, eds., *Steven Holl: Simmons Hall* (New York: Princeton Architectural Press, 2004), p. 25.

50 Extract from Steven Holl's 1998 master plan text.

52 Gannon and Denison, *Steven Holl: Simmons Hall,* p. 39.

54 Gannon and Denison, *Steven Holl: Simmons Hall,* pp. 57–60.

55 Gannon and Denison, *Steven Holl: Simmons Hall,* p. 97.

58 Gannon and Denison, *Steven Holl: Simmons Hall,* p. 108.

59 Gannon and Denison, *Steven Holl: Simmons Hall,* p. 114.

62 Wasserman Forum transcript.

66 Wasserman Forum transcript.

71 Quoted in an interview published in Mildred Friedman, ed., *Gehry Talks* (New York: Rizzoli, 1999), p. 280.

72 Transcript of an interview by Spencer Reiss for *Wired* magazine. The resulting article appeared as Spencer Reiss, "Frank Gehry's Geek Palace," *Wired* 12, no. 5 (May 2004).

73 MIT campus planning charette transcript.

74 Wasserman Forum transcript.

75 MIT campus planning charette transcript.

79 MIT campus planning charette transcript.

80 Wasserman Forum transcript.

83 MIT campus planning charette transcript.

85 Wasserman Forum transcript.

87 From a telephone interview, February 11, 2005.

88 Unpublished essay on the design of the Brain and Cognitive Sciences Complex.

90 Telephone interview.

93 Unpublished essay.

99 Telephone interview.

102 Fumihiko Maki, "Conception, Expression, Construction, the Third Pietro Belluschi Lecture, Autumn 1995," in Stanford Anderson, ed., *The Pietro Belluschi Lectures* (Cambridge: MIT School of Architecture and Planning, 1999), p. 12.

107 Maki, "Conception, Expression, Construction," p. 11.

117 Maki, "Conception, Expression, Construction," p. 16.

127 Transcript of interview by Reiss for *Wired.*

129 Wasserman Forum transcript.

BIBLIOGRAPHY

Brand, Stewart. *How Buildings Learn: What Happens after They're Built*. New York: Viking Penguin, 1994.

Brand, Stewart. *The Media Lab: Inventing the Future at MIT*. New York: Viking, 1987.

Chapman, M. Perry. *American Places: In Search of the Twenty-First Century Campus*. Westport: Praeger, 2006.

Dober, Richard. *Campus Planning*. New York: Reinhold, 1968.

Friedman, Mildred, ed. *Gehry Talks: Architecture + Process*. New York: Rizzoli, 2002.

Gannon, Todd, and Michael Denison, eds. *Steven Holl: Simmons Hall*. New York: Princeton Architectural Press, 2004.

Jarzombek, Mark. *Designing MIT: Bosworth's New Tech*. Boston: Northeastern University Press, 2004.

Joyce, Nancy E. *Building Stata: The Design and Construction of Frank O. Gehry's Stata Center at MIT*. Cambridge: MIT Press, 2004.

Kerr, Clark. *The Uses of the University*. 5th ed. Cambridge: Harvard University Press, 2001.

Muthesius, Stefan. *The Post-War University: Utopianist Campus and College*. New Haven: Paul Mellon Center for Studies in British Art, 2001.

O'Neal, William Bainter. *Jefferson's Buildings at the University of Virginia*. Charlottesville: University Press of Virginia, 1960.

Pelkonen, Eeva-Liisa, and Donald Albrecht (editors). *Eero Saarinen: Shaping the Future*. New Haven: Yale University Press, 2006.

Pollack, Sidney (director). *Sketches of Frank Gehry* (DVD). Sony Pictures Classics, 2006

Prescott, Samuel C. *When MIT Was "Boston Tech," 1861–1916*. Cambridge: Technology Press, 1954.

Ragheb, J. Fiona, ed. *Frank Gehry, Architect*. New York: Harry N. Abrams, 2003.

Rappolt, Mark, and Robert Violette, eds. *Gehry Draws*. Cambridge: MIT Press, 2004.

Ratti, Carlo, and Talia Dorsey, eds. *Inside the Sponge: Catalogue of the Exhibition at the Canadian Center for Architecture, 10 August–19 November 2006*. Montreal: Canadian Center for Architecture, 2006.

Rhodes, Frank H. T. *The Creation of the Future: The Role of the American University*. Ithaca: Cornell University Press, 2001.

Simha, O. Robert. *MIT Campus Planning, 1960–2000: An Annotated Chronology*. Cambridge: MIT, Office of the Executive Vice President, 2001.

Stratton, Julius A., and Loretta H. Mannix. *Mind and Hand: The Birth of MIT*. Cambridge: MIT Press, 2005.

Turner, Paul Venable. *Campus: An American Planning Tradition*. Cambridge: MIT Press, 1987.

Vest, Charles M. *The American Research University from World War II to World Wide Web*. Berkeley: University of California Press, 2007.

Vest, Charles M. *Pursuing the Endless Frontier: Essays on MIT and the Role of Research Universities*. Cambridge: MIT Press, 2004.

White, Pepper. *The Idea Factory: Learning to Think at MIT*. Cambridge: MIT Press, 2001 (reprint).

Williams, Rosalind H. *Retooling: A Historian Confronts Technological Change*. Cambridge: MIT Press, 2002.

Wylie, Francis E. *MIT in Perspective: A Pictorial History of the Massachusetts Institute of Technology*. Boston: Little, Brown, 1975.

ILLUSTRATION CREDITS

INTRODUCTION

1. Map adapted from the online MIT campus map maintained by the MIT Publishing Services Bureau.

1. THE AMERICAN CAMPUS

1. From *A Map of the State of Virginia Reduced from the Nine Sheet Map of the State, in Conformity to Law,* by Herman Böÿe; engraved by H. S. Tanner and E. B. Dawson (Richmond, c. 1827). Special Collections, University of Virginia Library.

2. WILLIAM WELLES BOSWORTH: TAYLORISM AND CLASSICISM

1–12. MIT Archives.
13. Courtesy of Venturi, Scott Brown and Associates, Inc.

3. POSTWAR PRAGMATISM

1. MIT Archives.
2. MIT Museum Radiation Laboratory Collection.
3–4. Courtesy of MIT Museum.

4. ALVAR AALTO AND EERO SAARINEN: MIDCENTURY MODERNISM

1. MIT Archives.
2–3, 8–13. Courtesy of MIT Museum.
4–5. Ezra Stoller © Esto.
6. TIME Magazine © 2007 Time Inc. Reprinted by permission.
7. Eero Saarinen Papers; Manuscripts and Archives, Yale University Library.

5. KEVIN ROCHE: ZESIGER SPORTS AND FITNESS CENTER

1–5. Courtesy of Kevin Roche John Dinkeloo and Associates LLC.
6–7. Andy Ryan.
8. MIT Archives.

6. STEVEN HOLL: SIMMONS HALL

1, 6 (three photographs), 8–9, 10 (photograph), 11. Andy Ryan.
2. MIT Archives.
3–5, 6 (sketches), 7, 10 (model). Steven Holl Architects.
6 (photograph at lower right), 12. Guy Hoffman, 2006.

7. FRANK GEHRY: STATA CENTER

1, 13, 15. Andy Ryan.
2. MIT Archives.
3–7, 12, 14. Gehry Partners.
8–11. Gehry Technologies.
16. Olin Partnership.
17. Guy Hoffman, 2006.

8. CHARLES CORREA: BRAIN AND COGNITIVE SCIENCES COMPLEX

1. Originally published in *House & Garden*.
2–3, 4 (computer graphics and model), 5 (drawing), 6, 7 (sketches and computer graphic), 9 (site plan). Charles Correa Associates.
4 (photograph), 7 (photograph), 8, 10. Andy Ryan.
5 (photograph). David Conlon.
9 (street sketch). Courtesy of Carol R. Johnson Associates, Inc.

9. FUMIHIKO MAKI: MEDIA LABORATORY

1–9. © Maki and Associates.

10. PLANNING A CAMPUS IN REAL TIME

1. MIT Archives.

INDEX